47 48 49 50 **After Fifty**

OTHER MARKETING BOOKS FROM PMP

The Kids Market: *Myths & Realities*

Marketing to American Latinos, Part I

Marketing to American Latinos, Part II

The Mirrored Window: *Focus Groups from a Moderator's Point of View*

The Great Tween Buying Machine

Marketing Insights to Help Your Business Grow

Why People Buy Things They Don't Need

A Knight's Code of Business: *How to Achieve Character and Competence in the Corporate World*

India Business: *Finding Opportunities in this Big Emerging Market*

Moderating to the Max! *A Full-tilt Guide to Creative Focus Groups and Insightful Depth Interviews*

After Fifty

How the Baby Boom Will Redefine the Mature Market

Travel & Leisure
Fast Food
Apparel/Retail
Technology
Health
Financial Services

Edited by
Leslie M. Harris

PARAMOUNT MARKET PUBLISHING, INC.

Paramount Market Publishing, Inc.
301 S. Geneva Street, Suite 109
Ithaca, NY 14850
www.paramountbooks.com
Telephone: 607-275-8100; 888-787-8100   Facsimile: 607-275-8101

Publisher: James Madden
Editorial Director: Doris Walsh

Cataloging in Publication Data available
ISBN 0-9725290-2-0

Book design and composition: Paperwork

Contents

Foreword

Myth: Everyone knows about the baby boom. Everyone has heard everything there is to hear. Besides, now that baby boomers are on the downward slope of the hill of life, they are still numerous, but are becoming, well, less interesting.

Reality: Both misconceptions could cost a marketer dearly. They are also a little presumptuous. How can one claim to "know" 77 million people? There is always something new to learn.

As for the persistent myth that life ends after age 50, that's just plain age discrimination. Ironically, it may also be a state of affairs that boomers unwittingly bring upon themselves. In their eagerness to live up to their label as the youth generation, boomers—with the help of marketers, to be sure—have created a youth-oriented consumer mindset that is proving difficult to shift.

In the mid-1990s, the oldest baby boomers turned 50 and the youngest turned 30. Much was made of the fact that the generation that at one time didn't trust anyone over 30, was now over 30 itself. The boomers were the ones who never grew up and who refuse to grow old. Like any other generalization or stereotype, this characterization has perhaps a grain of truth, but little more. Maturing boomers are, by and large, mature people with a great deal of life experience under their (expanding) belts.

Be that as it may, as this powerful group of Americans moves into its most powerful years, it seems to be suffering the fate of its predecessors. Like lemmings tumbling into the apocryphal abyss, boomers entering their fifties find themselves in a marketing wasteland. They are either ignored or attended to with stereotypical attitudes. Everyone is gray-haired or bald and doesn't want to be. No one can program a

VCR, not to mention a cell phone. And no one ever, ever tries anything new unless it's related to their failing bodily functions. One is decrepit, a buffoon, or both.

Mass marketing does require a reasonable level of generalization. The grains of truth that support the above stereotypes are that people do become gray, and older people do tend to have less facility with new technology. Perhaps the biggest misconceptions have to do not with physical or other "facts" of later life but with what they *mean*. Take the case of technology. Some older adults are genuine technophobes; others are just uninterested in the newest gadgets.

The same could be said of any product or service category. Even among older adults, one size doesn't fit all. Never did, never will. And the baby boom in and approaching its fifties takes the complexities of the mature market to a whole new level.

This book outlines many of the key themes that differentiate the baby boom as a mature market compared with previous generations, as well as the attitudes and behavior that set maturing boomers apart from each other.

For example, people in their fifties experience many major life events. That has been true before now, but boomers are amplifying the pattern. Second marriages, second careers, second homes—boomers are doing even more of these. Yet many are still taking the same traditional life path their parents did; marriage and child rearing, followed by an empty nest that remains empty; career progression peaking in later years, followed by retirement.

Life events mean marketing opportunities. For mature boomers, these are not limited to getting new furniture when the kids move out and joining a golf club when they retire. They include new reasons and ways to consume the same products they always have. Older boomers have new motivations for using the internet and new demands of fast food restaurants.

Boomers have high expectations of everything. They have been indulged all their lives, mostly because of the economic prosperity that marked the second half of the twentieth century. The resulting mindset of self indulgence and instant gratification does not characterize every boomer, of course, but it may be the single most distinguishing trait of this generation. They want what they want, the way they want it, and they want it now. In pursuit of this ambition, they have amassed levels of debt that horrify their parents. Their spending patterns may yet save the economy, or trash it. In the meantime, marketers who want insights into reaching boomers today and tomorrow will find them in the chapters that follow.

   "Everyone talks about the weather, but nobody does anything about it." This timeless observation attributed to Mark Twain sums up the reason why we *do* need yet another book about the baby boom. Unlike Twain's alleged comment, however, it is possible to do much more than just talk about the maturing baby boom; marketers can actually *do* something about it.

DIANE CRISPELL
Editor-at-Large
RoperASW

1

An Introduction:
Connecting with the Boomers

Leslie M. Harris
Mature Marketing and Research

W hen baby boomers were in their early 20s and late teens, they were the segment to attract and sell. The marketing wisdom was that manufacturers and their agencies needed to concentrate their efforts on this segment if they were to prosper and grow in the 21st century. Unfortunately, marketers got used to the idea of pursuing the youth market. Although boomers now in their 40s and 50s, with the leading edge closer to age 60, are no longer "babies" many marketers still think they have to attract the youth market to succeed. However, the boomer market is a more important force now than in their youthful heyday. As you will see in the chapters that follow, they have more money and more influence than ever before.

The reality is that marketing to the boomers is more complex than it used to be because the whole concept of who the boomers are has become more complex. The mistake made by many companies and their advertising agencies is that they look upon the boomer market as a single group of consumers.

University of Massachusetts marketing professor, Charles Schewe, divides boomers into two groups: the Leading Edge, born from 1946 to 1955, who came of age in the 1960s, and the Trailing Edge, born from 1955 to 1965, who came of age in the 1970s. Due to gender-related differences in outlook, these two groups most likely should be

Mature Marketing and Research, 85 India Row, Suite 30A, Boston, MA 02110; 617-720-4158; mmrharris@aol.com.

considered as four. You will learn more about the demographics of boomers and see comparisons of boomers and other cohorts in chapter one.

In the same way that not every automobile is a Ford, not every member of the boomer generation is the same. It is a diverse group, consisting of multiple sub-groups, with each sub-group having its own wants and needs. It includes executives and professionals at the top of their earning power, as well as new retirees and people who are relatively new entrants to the labor force. It includes parents still involved in their grown or near-grown children's economic and educational problems, grandparents who are raising grandchildren, singles, and empty nesters. It includes people eager to embrace new trends and technologies as well as those wanting nothing to do with technology. The boomer market is at least as heterogeneous as any other major market segment and its internal divisions are deep.

The key to effective marketing to boomers is understanding that there are no segments or sub-groups that are descriptive of all segments.

The buying behavior of each sub-group varies with the economic conditions, social events, and technological advances that characterized the formative years of each. Age segments can be further defined by gender, labor force status, income, ethnicity, health, marital status, presence of children, and general lifestyle. Although the division between retired and not retired is important, individuals may have their own definition of retirement.

For example, if your target market is boomers in their early 50s, they probably still have children in college and are not retired. Or, you may target the boomer in her late 50s who is fully retired from career number one, and may be considering or working at a second occupation. Since many boomers have a completely different definition of retirement (discussed in Chapter 9), it is not a good idea to group retired boomers with people born before 1946.

Boomers are America's self-absorbed generation—restless, relentless, always showing off. For them, it wasn't enough to grow up, get married, become parents, be responsible, and get off the stage as their parents did. The boomers have to get in shape, protest the war, run a marathon, see a shrink, practice yoga, buy a boat, join a cult, learn to cook, and take karate. Boomers don't worry too much as long as they're having a good time. They want to feel alive, young, and vibrant. It is their stress management strategy, according to one boomer.

Boomers, says Peter Francese, the founder of *American Demographics* magazine, make their own rules. They have always acted in ways that are contrary to the behavior of the generation that preceded them. The difference is that they are smart and educated and know what they like. Many have a lot of money that translates into enormous buying power. Many are accomplished and spoiled and will receive —and leave—large inheritances.

Recent studies, discussed in the chapters that follow, have confirmed their willingness to try new products and to spend a greater share of their income on indulging themselves than any other segments of the population. As they age, they are spending even more on personal indulgences that range from health and beauty aids to help them look younger, to food products with extra nutritional value, and expensive cars to make them feel younger.

According to *Modern Maturity* magazine, those aged 50 to 59 show greater change in their priorities, product needs, brand preferences and criteria for selecting products than in any other decade of their lives. In fact, both qualitative and quantitative research indicates the 50s are a decade of great change. Longer life expectancy and awareness help to shape the attitudes of the boomer market. Gloria Steinem, turning 50, said it felt a lot like 40. Gail Sheehy called age 50 "a midpoint, not an endpoint." While the prospect of retirement still looms in the foreseeable future, Horace Deets, executive director of AARP calls it "no longer a withdrawal, but rather a transition." Nonetheless, the phrase "50 years" is fraught with ominous meanings. It is half a century, well past the halfway mark of almost everyone's life expectancy, and it indicates irrevocably that one has reached the downward slope of existence. Realizing chronological maturity conflicts with reluctance in letting go of the illusion of youth.

Starting in the Kennedy years, the great wave of boomers ironically boosted the marketing preference for youth. Youth is hip, cool, fun. Young people are more attractive than the old, and they live longer.

Marketers are forever hopeful that if they catch customers while they are young, they'll have them for life. Now this great wave is aging, and as advertising guru Jerry Della Femina put it, "When will Madison Avenue get it? There are consumers older than 50 and somebody will get rich discovering it."

The increase of models in their 50s shows that there has been some discovery by ad agencies that women at age 50 and beyond can be effective spokespersons. Proof is Anne Roberts, age 52, who was signed by Procter & Gamble to a six-figure TV and print campaign to pitch Oil of Olay's Pro Vital Skin Care Collection. Actress Jaclyn Smith, 51, has appeared in ads for Rembrandt's first mouthwash and toothpaste for older consumers.

One challenge that we continue to hear is that once someone reaches the mid-point in their lives, they are set in their ways in terms of brand preference. To test this belief, AARP and the RoperASW research organization conducted a survey of how adults at all ages think about brands. Some of the key findings indicate:

- Sixty-six percent of all consumers base their brand purchase decisions on "gives good value for the money"—not brand name.

- Sixty-eight percent of adults aged 45 to 55 typically research different brands before they make purchase decisions compared with 62 percent of consumers aged 45 and older.

- Seventy percent of consumers aged 45 and older will try (but not necessarily switch to) a new brand, if a person they trust recommends it.

- Contrary to the thinking of some marketers, about 50 percent of those aged 45 and over are always looking for better products, indicating that brand loyalty in many cases is more a function of the product category than of age. (See table opposite.)

Writes Maria Puente of *USA Today*, "Boomers used to have long hair; now they have receding hair. They used to be young and rebellious; now they're middle-aged and comfortable. They're reliving the good times. By day, they're respectable, with serious and important jobs. At night and on the weekends, they're revisiting their youthful fantasies. There are dentists; there are lawyers; there are editors and CEOs. There are members of the clergy—all boomers—all committed to having as good a time as possible."

FIGURE 1.1

Brand Loyalty

Percent who prefer one product brand or one service provider.

	Total	18–44	45–54	55–64	65+
Airlines	18%	18%	17%	22%	7%
Athletic footwear	29	35	23	28	20
Athletic/leisure wear	10	11	8	9	8
Auto insurance	70	63	76	78	80
Bath soap	49	46	53	55	50
Car-rental companies	19	21	19	20	12
Cars	46	43	48	51	56
Credit cards	27	23	25	32	39
DVD/Video players	24	27	23	18	22
Home stereo equipment	28	34	24	26	17
Hotels/motels	12	13	11	13	10
Large home appliances	35	31	40	39	40
Life insurance	41	35	46	42	55
SUVS/trucks/vans	38	39	39	40	30

Source: AARP and Roper Research

Ken DeCell, age 50, an editor at *Washingtonian* magazine plays guitar in a boomer band called The Developments. The band includes a lawyer, a dentist, a builder, and a direct-mail professional. He says, "We've discovered the joys of playing the golden oldies." Rabbi Steven Carr Reuben, age 52, who plays drums in a boomer band called the Jam in the Los Angeles area says, "It's a validation of that part of us that doesn't want to lose touch with our passions in life."

In 2005, boomers will range in age from 41 to 59. The U.S. Census Bureau projects a population of 69 million aged 50 to 59 by the year 2010, a growth of about 50 percent. Their size, approximately 28 percent of our total population, and the differences in who they believe they are necessitate careful attention by marketers.

Boomer icons like Timothy Leary, Marilyn Monroe, Alan Ginsburg, Mario Savio (Berkeley free speaker), author Jack Kerouac, Jerry Lee Lewis, Bob Dylan, and Elvis weren't boomers. Even the Beatles weren't boomers, but they set the pace, broke the mold, changed society although they belonged to the generation before the boomers, the group called the Silent Generation. You could consider them the vanguard of the boomers. Boomers picked their leaders from that generation and then raised the bar.

The Boomers Never Grew Up

Boomers can't grow up because they see age as a lifestyle choice rather than a chronological imperative and they choose to stay young.

The big difference between the boomers and the generations before them is that they never grew up. Their grandparents grew up. Their parents grew up, but boomers can't grow up because they see age as a lifestyle choice rather than a chronological imperative and they choose to stay young.

Now, many boomers have a home computer. Having a brokerage account is no big achievement. Boomers spend more money than they earn and carry more than one credit card. Vacations are just as likely to be on a cruise ship as to the nearby mountains or the local shore. The family car has become several cars, many of them made by Japanese, Swedish, and Korean companies. Cable and satellite systems bring hundreds of TV channels, and print media is fragmented into thousands of choices. Divorce and job jumping are endemic and the extended family is physically extended with brothers, sisters, moms and dads living thousands of miles apart. Life is fast, chaotic, and anything but predictable.

Boomers Are the "Driven" Generation

David Kiley, in a lead article in *USA Today,* reports that many boomer households are adding their third or fourth cars, often something for fun. Alan Hall of Ford Motors special vehicle team believes money and variety are driving the trends; he says "more disposable income, particularly among the aging, but fun loving boomer." There are lots of nests empty of kids for the first time, a lot of mid-life crises, a lot of early retirements with big payoffs, and a lot of inheritances being realized from their World War II parents. It all adds up to extra cars and cars that are more toy and indulgence than mere conveyance.

We now have a generation of buyers who are able to be a bit more selfish and indulge themselves, who are healthier and more optimistic, and who see getting old as an option rather than a sentence.

Richard Lentinello, Executive Editor of *Hemmings Motor News*, says that boomers are searching the market for vintage cars. They are gravitating to those cars either because they were too young to drive or could not afford them when they were new. As one boomer said, "I feel really good when I get into my 1962 Corvette because it brings back memories of my youth and it's fun."

Carol Morgan of Strategic Directions Group describes 40-to-54-year-olds as people who "check out *Consumer Reports* before buying." They are people who are expressing themselves through their cars, and they don't care if it is the highest quality or easiest to repair.

Joe Queenan in his book about boomers: *Balsamic Dreams: A Short But Self-Important History of the Baby Boomer Generation*, (Henry Holt and Company, New York, 2001) writes: "The way history will view the Boomers. They had immense youthful promise. They showed occasional flashes of genius. But poor judgment and a number of serious character flaws prevented them from achieving true greatness. They could have been contenders. But in the end, they didn't have what it takes."

In a 2002 television commercial, a young contestant is asked to spell "microphone." She barely gets to "M–I–C" before a boomer adult butts in with "K–E–Y." The boomer audience beams and joins in, chanting M–O–U–S–E. This poor kid has to stand there and listen to grownups steal her moment while they sing the theme song from *The Mickey Mouse Club,* now used to promote vacations to Disneyland. That's the boomers for you! Self-centered and still kids!

Nevertheless, the boomers are savvy. With all their money and enormous buying power, they represent an important market that requires creative planning and research in effectively marketing to them.

As Susan Crandall, editor of *More* magazine, wrote: "Boomers are the richest demographic group so they should be front and center in calls to buy. . . . Still much of the time America remains mired in a youth culture. We continue to see a constant stream of 20-somethings in magazines and on TV, decorating ads for products from suits to sedans."

Despite the continuing emphasis on marketing to youth, the 45-to-64 age group will account for the highest share of consumer spending in the coming decade and beyond. Now let's look at a more detailed portrait of the boomers and the generations that came before and after them.

2

The Baby Boom:
A Demographic Portrait

Theodore L. Reed
ReedHaldyMcIntosh & Associates

Historically most consumer marketing has focused on the life-stage-based needs and priorities of the retail public. Realistically, it is plausible to expect that those who are leaving school and entering the job market are likely to have different consumption patterns and consumer preferences than those who are at the early stages of family formation. Similarly, it has been demonstrated that those in the process of raising children have different needs and perspectives than those who have completed child rearing and are building their lives around an empty nest. Finally, as we watch the members of the baby boom move from being empty nesters toward retirement, we can anticipate yet another set of consumer priorities and consumption patterns.

> **Cohort**
> A group of individuals having a statistical factor (as age or class membership) in common in a demographic study.
> —*Webster's New Collegiate Dictionary*

While recognizing the importance of life-stage changes, however, it has become increasingly clear that important cohort-related differences have an impact on the consumer preferences and consumption patterns of the Leading Edge and Trailing Edge baby boomers. As each new cohort ages, moving through the typical life stages from early adulthood on to retirement, it brings with it a new perspective and a new set of formative experiences that shape its consumer behavior and preferences.

Theodore L. Reed is a partner in ReedHaldyMcIntosh & Associates, 600 North Jackson Street, Media, PA 19063; 610-565-8715 X103; treed@rhmassociates.com, www.rhmassociates.com

Sociologists have long been aware of the importance of the cohort phenomenon in understanding social behavior. Karl Mannheim, one of these observers, noted that "belonging to the same generation or age group" endows those who belong "with a common location in the social and historical process . . . predisposing them for a certain characteristic mode of thought and experience, and a characteristic type of historically relevant action."

As a result of these social and historical experiences, the Leading Edge and Trailing Edge boomer cohorts have a different perspective on the world than do the Postwar cohort that preceded them or the Gen-X cohort that follows them. This book demonstrates to marketers that there are advantages in crafting a new approach to each new cohort rather than replicating the approach taken to the previous cohort. It outlines the benefits of attempting to understand the lifestyle and behavioral differences that will affect each new cohort. It identifies the consumer behavior, responses to goods and services in the marketplace and to the promotion of those goods and services that are unique, especially for the Leading Edge and Trailing Edge boomer cohorts.

This chapter outlines some of the underlying changes which will determine the content and approach of successful marketing campaigns directed toward Leading Edge and Trailing Edge cohorts of the generation collectively known as baby boomers. It focuses on some of the lifestyle and behavioral differences between these two cohorts, demonstrating how they differ from those who preceded them (Postwar generation) and those who follow (Gen X).

Many of these differences are rooted in the demographic composition of these cohorts, especially the jump in the sheer numbers compared with earlier cohorts. Compared with the Postwar group, unparalleled economic prosperity encountered by the two baby-boomer cohorts had an impact on their lifestyles and expectations. Other differences are the result of unique historical experiences faced by these groups during their formative years, but the specific impact of these events is often harder to document and forecast.

Our focus is on four cohorts whenever possible. The differences between the two baby boomer cohorts (Leading Edge and Trailing Edge) are the core. However, an understanding of how to market to these two cohorts requires a comparison with the preceding and following cohorts—Postwar and Generation X. Because of the difficulty

of finding appropriate time series data, many of the cohort comparisons are between adjoining cohorts, rather than among all four cohorts.
Nevertheless, it is possible to paint a detailed picture of the Leading
Edge and Trailing Edge boomers that augments our understanding of
their potential as customers and their uniqueness as recipients of marketing efforts.

The Four Cohorts Defined

Figure 2.1 on page 12 identifies the birth dates for each of the four
cohorts. It also defines the formative years for each cohort, those years
between ages 17 and 23 when basic ideas, perspectives and worldview
are imprinted leaving an impact on the members of the cohort throughout their lives.

As marketers, we know that different life stages have a major influence on the focus of our consumption patterns. However, life-stage
experiences are different for each cohort. To understand the impact of
cohort identity, we must examine how each cohort responds at each
stage of life (age). The interaction between cohort and life-stage experiences provides the foundation for understanding how to target these
two boomer cohorts as they age.

Figure 2.2 on page 13 traces the four cohorts (Postwar, Leading
Edge boomer, Trailing Edge boomer and Gen X) through the various
life stages, showing the age of each cohort during the years for which
we have been able to collect comparative data on behavior and lifestyles.
For example, for each decade, 1970 through 2000, one cohort was
going through the 25-to-34-year-old life stage, typically the period of
early adulthood and family formation. Looking ahead, we are interested in understanding how the experiences of the Leading Edge
boomers differed from those of the Postwar generation as they went
through the 45-to-54-year-old life stage. We hope to use these insights
to anticipate how the Leading Edge boomer cohort will respond to
the next life stage. Similarly, we are interested in understanding the differences between the behavior and lifestyle of the Trailing Edge
boomers and the Leading Edge boomers as they went through the ages
of 35 to 44. Again, the objective is to gain insight into how the Trailing Edge boomers will compare during their mid-forties and mid-fifties
with the Leading Edge boomers, who went through that life stage during the last decade.

FIGURE 2.1
Cohort Definitions: Birth Dates & Dates of Formative Experiences

Birth dates ☐ Formative years ■

Year	Postwar cohort	Leading Edge boomer cohort	Trailing Edge boomer cohort	Generation X cohort	Milestone Events, Defining Moments
1935					
1936					
1937					
1938					
1939					
1940					
1941					Pearl Habor attacked
1942					
1943					
1944					
1945					End of World War II
1946					
1947					
1948					
1949					
1950					Election of Eisenhower
1951					Korean War (1950–1953)
1952					
1953					Good economic times (1950s)
1954					McCarthyism (1950–1954)
1955					
1956					Suburban growth
1957					Sputnik
1958					
1959					
1960					Cold War (1950s–1970s)
1961					Emergence of rock-n-roll
1962					Civil rights movement
1963					John F. Kennedy assassination
1964					War on Poverty
1965					
1966					
1967					Vietnam War (1964–1973)
1968					R.F.K. and M.L.K. assassinations
1969					First man on the moon
1970					Kent State killings
1971					
1972					Watergate (1972–1974)
1973					Stock market slide (1973–1975)
1974					Nixon resignation
1975					Fall of Vietnam
1976					
1977					
1978					Energy crisis
1979					
1980					
1981					Reaganomics (1981–1989)
1982					
1983					
1984					
1985					
1986					Challenger explosion
1987					Stock market crash
1988					AIDS crisis (late 1980s–)
1989					Fall of the Berlin Wall
1990					
1991					Gulf War
1992					
1993					Good economic times (1990s)
1994					
1995					Internet takes off (1995–)
1996					
1997					

FIGURE 2.2

Cohort Ages by Year

Cohort	1970	1980	1990	2000	2010
Postwar	25-34	36-44	45-54	55-64	65-74
Leading Edge Boomers	15-24	25-34	36-44	45-54	55-64
Trailing Edge Boomers		15-24	25-34	36-44	45-54
Generation X			15-24	25-34	36-44

Meredith, Schewe and Karlovich provide a snapshot of each of the four cohorts in their pioneering book *Defining Markets, Defining Moments* (Hungry Minds, 2000). The snapshots for each of the four cohorts, drawing upon their insights, are shown in Figure 2.4 overleaf.

Cohort Size

The understanding of the lifestyle and behavioral differences between the Leading Edge and Trailing Edge boomers begins with an examination of the size of these two cohorts.

Cohort size demands attention

The most impressive feature of the two baby boomer cohorts is their sheer size compared with the preceding Postwar cohort (and even the following Gen X cohort). The size of these two groups alone means that they cannot be ignored, for combined they represented about 30 percent of the total population of the United States in 2000 and controlled almost 75 percent of the personal wealth of the nation. Moreover, the size of the two baby boomer cohorts makes it possible for consumer marketers to tailor products and

FIGURE 2.3

Relative Cohort Sizes, 2000
in millions

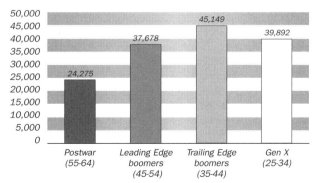

FIGURE 2.4

Postwar Cohort	Leading Edge Boomer Cohort
Age in 2002: 56–66	Age in 2002: 47–56
Population: 22 million, 8%	Population: 36 million, 13%
Key values and concerns	**Key values and concerns**
The American Dream	*Personal and social expression*
Conformity	Protected individualism
Stability	Youth
Family	Health and wellness
Self-fulfillment	
Current and next life stage	**Current and next life stage**
Divorce and remarriage for some	Empty nesting
Empty nesting	Child rearing
Grandparenting	Some grandparenting
Eldercare	Second career
Retirement	Divorce
Retirement communities	
Emotions and affinities	**Emotions and affinities**
Desire experiences, not things	Nostalgia
Enjoying life	Rebellious
Changing roles for women	Social justice
Nostalgic	Generational community
Sexually repressed	Sexually experimental
Physiographic profile	**Physiographic profile**
Chronic medical conditions	Vision problems
Aches and pains	Weight changes
Changing body structure	Hypertension
Vision and hearing loss	Arthritis
Memory loss	Gray hair and hair loss
From looking good to feeling good	Menopause
Social Activities and Lifestyles	**Social Activities and Lifestyles**
Travel	Exercise
Family and grandchildren	Leisure a necessity
Volunteerism	
Purchasing behavior	**Purchasing behavior**
Spend some, save some	Plastic surgery
Internet	Big spenders
	Convenience is a key

Trailing Edge Boomer Cohort

Age in 2002: 38–47
Population: 42 million, 15%

Gen X Cohort

Age in 2002: 27– 36
Population: 34 million, 12%

Key values and concerns
Lonely individualism
Cynicism and distrust of government
Health and wellness
Family commitments

Key values and concerns
Free agency and independence
Friendships important
Acceptance of violence and sex
Street smart
Pursuit of quality of life
Cynical about the future

Current and next life stage
Home ownership
Child rearing into teenage years
Divorce and remarriage
Career changes

Current and next life stage
Graduate school
Career search
Cohabitation
Marriage
Home ownership
First child

Emotions and affinities
Informal
Politically ambivalent
Overtly materialistic
Sexually liberated

Emotions and affinities
Environmental concerns
Social, sexual and ethnic diversity
Sexually cautious
Global community

Physiographic profile
First markers of aging
Acute health conditions

Physiographic profile
Invincible
Earliest signs of aging

Social Activities and Lifestyles
Physical fitness
Possession experiences

Social Activities and Lifestyles
Drinking with friends
Technology oriented
Alternative religions

Purchasing behavior
Feeling deprived
Convenience
Appeal to young kids
Price and value

Purchasing behavior
Price conscious
Internet buyers
Credit card users

Source: *Defining Markets, Defining Moments,* by Geoffrey E. Meredith and Charles E. Schewe, Ph.D. with Janice Karlovich, © 2002, Hungry Minds, Inc., New York, NY. Used by permission.

services to reflect the particular tastes and preferences of different segments within the cohorts.

Increase in scale is not enough.

The 60+ percent increase in the cohort size from the Postwar cohort to the Leading Edge boomer cohort immediately attracted social attention. Multiple institutions struggled to provide services to this initial group of boomers as they overwhelmed existing capacity of the institutions that dealt with them at each stage of their lives. Today, the parts of the economy addressing the needs of aging boomers are still attempting to forecast the likely impact of the onrushing age wave. At the same time they need to understand that the goods and services demanded by this group are not the same goods and services delivered in the same way as those provided for the Postwar and earlier generations.

The dramatic impact of the Leading Edge boomers, moreover, was followed by another 15 percent increase in births from the Leading Edge boomers to the Trailing Edge boomers. This continued, though slower, growth forced the same institutions to react again to the pressure of producing for and serving dramatically increasing numbers. And again, as they age, it is becoming clearer that the goods and services demanded by the Trailing Edge boomers are not necessarily identical to those required for the Leading Edge boomer cohort. Again, increase in scale alone is not a sufficient response for a successful enterprise.

Cohort Incomes

Cohort experiences and expectations are not the same

As dramatic as the population changes have been and continue to be, the impact on the economy and on various institutions is not a function of size alone. The issue is more complicated. Boomers are different from the Postwar generation in other ways and Leading Edge boomers and Trailing Edge boomers are quite different from each other. These differences are rooted both in cohort size and in differences in their cohort-based experiences, as reflected in a number of demographic and economic indicators.

Comparable age incomes are higher

The average (mean) incomes of Leading Edge boomers are more than 10 percent higher than those of the Postwar cohort at the same age (in constant 2000 dollars) and the pattern of higher incomes for later cohorts is repeated. On average, a cohort's wage income increases with age.

FIGURE 2.5

Income of Wage Earners at Comparable Ages

by cohort, in standardized 2000 dollars

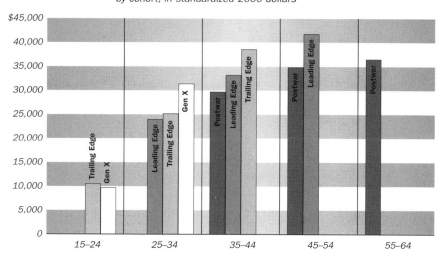

The trend toward higher wages with each successive cohort is consistent over time, suggesting new marketing opportunities as income increases. However, three variations in this pattern necessarily produce differences in the behavior and lifestyles of the Leading Edge boomers vs. the Trailing Edge boomers.

• Paired cohort average income growth slows for later cohorts.

Trailing Edge boomers have significantly lower income growth rates compared with their previous (Leading Edge boomer) cohort, and the growth rate in average income falls again slightly for Gen X cohort pairs.

FIGURE 2.6

Average Percentage Increases in Income
Compared with Previous Cohort

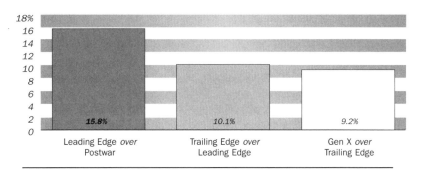

Leading Edge *over* Postwar	Trailing Edge *over* Leading Edge	Gen X *over* Trailing Edge

Why is this difference important to marketers? The impact of the baby boomer cohorts has been two fold. First has been the increase in the cohort size. Second, and equally important, has been the increase in purchasing power (wage income) of the baby boomers compared with those who preceded them. The figure above makes clear that it is not realistic to expect continued increases in incomes for successive cohorts. Average income growth is lower for Trailing Edge boomers and slower still for Gen Xers as they reach the same ages. Overall, this translates into less purchasing-power growth and less discretionary-income growth for each successive cohort.

- *Income increases vary significantly with the overall health of the economy.*

Wages for all cohorts increased more in the 1990s than in the 1980s. However, the increases are not spread equally across all age groups and hence have a varied impact on the purchasing power of different cohorts. In general, average income increases for younger people are more impacted by economic cycles than are the incomes of older people.

When the economy is growing slowly, as during the 1980s, paired cohort increases were smaller overall. In addition, the paired cohort average wage increases were increasingly smaller for later cohorts, even to the point where Gen Xers experienced negative income growth compared with Trailing Edge boomers during the 1980s. When the economy is growing rapidly, as it did during the 1990s, wage increases are higher for younger people, those in the Trailing Edge and Gen Xer cohorts, as shown in Figure 2.7 below. Gen Xers have the greatest paired cohort growth, and Leading Edge boomers have the smallest paired cohort growth.

FIGURE 2.7

Impact of the Economy on Income Increases
Compared with Previous Cohort

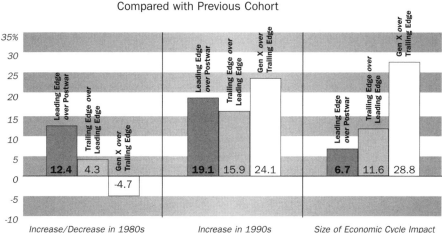

Marketers are well aware that boom times have a positive impact across all markets. This analysis, in addition, demonstrates that the largest proportional increases (and decreases) occur among those in the youngest age groups and, hence, among later cohorts. During successful times, marketers can expect the greatest increases in demand among those who are younger. Conversely, those targeting Leading Edge boomers will continue to find a population with higher income gains and less income fluctuation based on the economic cycle.

- *Wage income increases are increasingly concentrated among the highest paid.*

Wage income increases for the Trailing Edge boomer and Gen-X cohorts are substantially more concentrated among the highest paid.

Examining the mean vs. median wage increases among paired cohorts reveals this trend. The mean, which sums all wages and divides by the total number of wage earners, gives proportionally greater weight to higher incomes. The median—the point at which half the wage earners have higher and half have lower incomes—is a calculation that gives equal weight to all wage earners, no matter how high or low their incomes.

The *inequality* in the distribution of wage increases is most notable among Trailing Edge boomers. They are sandwiched between the Leading Edge boomers who were relatively unaffected by the swings in the economy of the 1980s and 1990s and the Gen Xers whose wage income increases (by both mean and median measures) were dramatic during the 1990s. These results are shown in figure 2.8 below:

FIGURE 2.8

Distribution of Wage Income Increases
by Cohort Pairs, 1980–2000

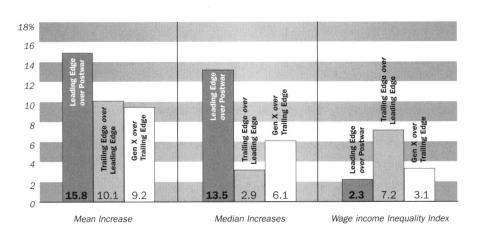

These trends alert marketers to changing market opportunities. Once marketers start to look beyond the Leading Edge boomers to the Trailing Edge boomers and Gen X cohorts, the product mix needs to increasingly reflect changes in the distribution of income within the cohorts which are skewing wage income increases toward upper income members of each successive cohort.

Cohorts and Age Distributions

The combined Leading Edge boomer and Trailing Edge boomer cohorts have been described as a bulge moving through a python that has just consumed a particularly large meal. Compared with the Post-war cohort, the dramatic impact of seeing these cohorts move through different ages with each decade, is to understand the impact of sheer numbers. It is important for marketers to understand that the size of the Trailing Edge boomer cohort is larger than that of the Leading Edge boomers. In addition, it is important to understand that although the Gen X cohort is smaller than that of the Trailing Edge boomers, it is still equivalent in size to that of the Leading Edge boomers. In the coming decade, the large group of Leading Edge boomers will be moving into their late 50s and early 60s. Trailing Edge boomers will be moving into their late 40s and early 50s. Moreover, those "youthful" Gen Xers will be aging into their late 30s and early 40s.

FIGURE 2.9

Cohort Aging, 1980–2000

cohort size in age ranges, in millions

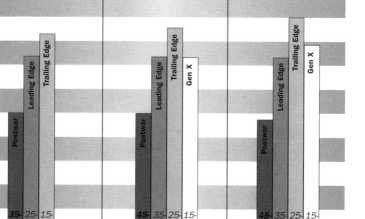

Cohorts and Gender

The percentage of females decreases slightly with each successive cohort when you compare the percentage of females at each distinct age. For the Leading Edge boomer and Trailing Edge boomer cohorts, however, this difference is likely to be erased by the increasing proportions of females at each age grouping, the result of higher male mortality.

Cohorts and Race/Ethnic Distributions

Census information on the racial/ethnic composition of the population at various ages indicates that the experiences of the boomer cohorts are significantly different from those in the Postwar cohort.

FIGURE 2.10

Percent of Population Classified as White

by cohort age

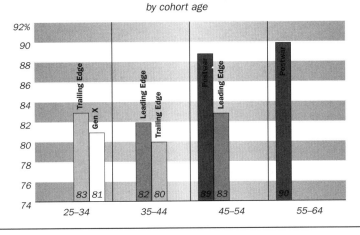

First, the proportion of each age group that is classified as white drops significantly from the Postwar cohort to the Leading Edge boomer cohort, from 89 percent white to 83 percent white. The percentages for the two boomer cohorts, stay relatively similar, in the low 80 percent range, as do those for the Gen X cohort.

Second, the proportion classified as white for Trailing Edge boomer cohort drops from when the cohort was aged 25 to 34 (83 percent) to when the cohort was aged 35 to 44 (80 percent). This is a reflection of increased Latin American and Asian immigration, beginning in the 1970s, but does not reflect those Hispanic immigrants who are classified as white in the census. The new immigrants are younger, so there is no discernable impact on the Leading Edge boomer cohort, which was already older by the time immigration from Latin America and Asia increased. In addition, these data reflect national averages, and we would expect that the patterns would be more pronounced in the West, Southwest, and in large metropolitan areas, which have been the destinations for many of the new immigrants. Trailing Edge boomers are more likely to have experience in multi-racial and multi-cultural settings than are the Leading Edge boomers. In addition, they are more likely to be competing in the job, educational, and housing markets with new groups of immigrants.

Finally, it is clear that the immigration patterns are likely to affect Gen Xers even more than Trailing Edge boomers. Ages 25 to 34 is the only group for which we have comparative data. The proportion of that age group classified as white (again excluding Hispanics who are classified as white) is somewhat lower for Gen Xers (83 percent vs. 81 percent) than it was for those in the preceding Trailing Edge boomer cohort.

Cohorts and Household Composition

Census data provide us with several insights into changing household composition as you look at how the various cohorts behave at comparable ages.

Percent married declines slightly

The proportion of those at each age who are married does not change significantly as one compares one cohort to the next. We do find a slight decrease in the proportion who report that they are married in the 45-to-54 age group when comparing the Postwar and the Leading Edge boomer cohorts (from 74 percent to 71 percent). Comparing Leading Edge and Trailing Edge boomers in the group aged 35 to 44, we find that the proportion who is married is nearly identical. Comparing Trailing Edge and Gen X cohorts at the age of 25 to 34, we see a drop in the proportion who are married. Again, however, the decrease from 57 percent to 55 percent is small compared with some of the other behavioral indicators that we have examined in this chapter.

Percent never married increases for younger cohorts

The proportion that is unmarried reveals greater differences between cohort behavior than does the data on the percent that are married.

FIGURE 2.11

Never Marrieds

percent by age

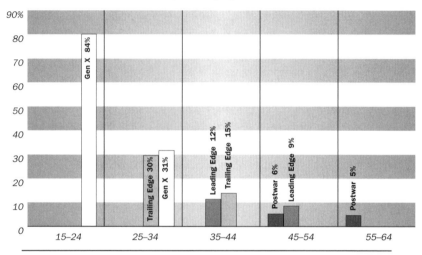

Comparing the Postwar and the Leading Edge cohorts, we find that the proportion who never married during the 45 to 54 ages is 50 percent higher among the latter group, a difference of 6 percent vs. 9 percent. A similar percentage difference exists among those aged 35 to 44, where we find that 15 percent of the Trailing Edge cohort has never married, compared with 12 percent of the Leading Edge cohort, a difference of 25 percent. Those aged 25 to 34, also differ slightly on this behavior from the Trailing Edge cohort to those in Gen X, and again, the pattern is that the later cohort has a slightly higher proportion who are never married than its predecessor cohort.

Cohorts and Educational Attainment

A comparison of the levels of educational achievement of Leading Edge and Trailing Edge boomer cohorts generally reveals that the proportions who have complete high school or higher and college or higher are quite similar for the two cohorts. Both cohorts differ significantly in level of educational achievement from the Postwar cohort, and they appear to be quite different from the Gen X cohort in the proportion who have completed college or more.

The proportions of the Leading Edge boomers who have completed high school at each age is significantly higher than the comparable proportions for those in the Postwar generation.

FIGURE 2.12

High School Graduates

percent by age

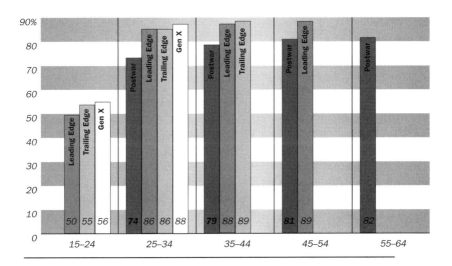

The increase in the proportion completing high school or more is most noticeable as each cohort reaches the 25-to-34 age group. For this age group, the proportion completing high school increases with each successive cohort. The proportion jumps from 74 percent for the Postwar cohort to 86 percent for the Leading Edge boomers. The proportion completing high school or more is the same for Trailing Edge boomers at the same age, 86 percent, and it rises only slightly to 88 percent for the Gen Xers.

By the time each cohort reaches ages 35 to 44, the differences are not as sharp. The proportion of the Postwar cohort completing a high school education or more has increased to 79 percent, while the comparable increases for the Leading Edge boomers is to 88 percent and to 89 percent for the Trailing Edge boomers. However, the income data reported above shows that the baby boom cohorts have had greater employment opportunities because of their educational attainment. A somewhat more dramatic change in educational attainment is apparent among those who have completed a college education or more, again comparing those in similar ages. From these data, we see evidence of a couple of behavioral changes that are likely to have an impact on consumption patterns and marketing for each of the two boomer cohorts.

Both Leading Edge and Trailing Edge boomers show a 50 percent increase in the proportion completing college or more compared with the Postwar Cohort.

FIGURE 2.13

Undergraduate and Graduate Degree-holders

percent by age

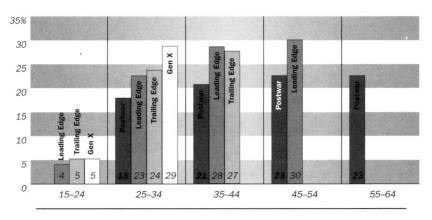

In the 25-to-34 year age group, we again see that the proportions are significantly higher for the Leading Edge and Trailing Edge boomer cohorts, compared with those in the Postwar cohort. The proportions who have completed college or more by the time they reach age 34 jumps dramatically from 16 percent for the Postwar cohort to 23 percent for the Leading Edge boomers and 24 percent for the Trailing Edge boomers, a rise of almost 50 percent. For Gen X, it rises again to 28 percent.

The absolute gap in educational achievement from the Postwar to the Leading Edge boomer generation decreases slightly by the time people in each generation reach the ages 35 to 44. For the Postwar generation, 21 percent have completed college or better by this time. For the Leading Edge boomers, the proportion has increased by 5 percent to 28 percent. For the Trailing Edge boomers, the number has increased substantially less, from 24 percent to 27 percent, somewhat surprising, given the state of the economy during the 1990s when the Trailing Edge boomers were going through these years.

Cohorts and Home Ownership

The proportions of home ownership, unlike other behavioral patterns observed for these four cohorts do not change significantly between the two baby boomer cohorts and the Postwar cohort that preceded them. Apart from constant increases in home ownership with age, the differences between pairs of cohorts at the same age are generally within a couple of percentage points. The one notable exception is for Gen X, whose experience during the economic good times of the 1990s resulted in a home ownership rate 3 percent higher at age 25 to 34 than was true for the Trailing Edge boomers.

FIGURE 2.14

Home Ownership

percent by age

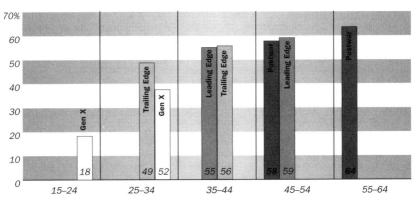

Cohorts and Their Geographic Distribution

The geographic distribution of the four cohorts at similar ages shows slight shifts from the earlier cohorts to the later ones. Not surprisingly, they reflect the general population shift from the Northeast and the Midwest to the South and West.

Leading Edge boomers more concentrated in South than Postwar cohort

Leading Edge boomers have slightly smaller representations in the Northeast and the Midwest than do those at the same age from the Postwar cohort. Correspondingly, the proportion of Leading Edge boomers who are living in the South is somewhat higher, and the same pattern is found in the somewhat higher proportions of Leading Edge boomers in the West, compared with those in the Postwar cohorts at the same age.

FIGURE 2.15

Percent Distribution by Region at Age 45–54

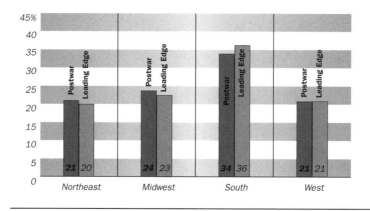

Smaller proportions of Trailing Edge boomers live in the Northeast and the Midwest

When comparing Trailing Edge boomers to the Leading Edge boomers, the regional distribution shift is in the same direction and magnitude as the pattern observed for the differences between the Postwar and Leading Edge boomers. Again, we observe a slight shift in the proportions of the later cohort (at the same age) toward residence in the South, and the West.

FIGURE 2.16

Percent Distribution by Region at Age 35–44

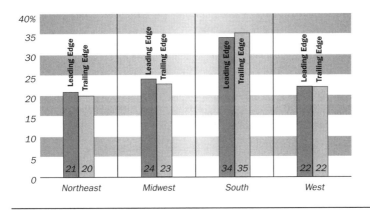

Gen Xers shift to the South and West more pronounced than for earlier cohorts

The residential shift of Gen Xers from the Northeast and the Midwest to the South and the West continues the pattern seen in earlier same-age group comparisons for earlier cohorts. Westward movement is again in evidence for Gen Xers, for whom 24 percent live in the West at the age of 25 to 34 compared with 22 percent of the Trailing Edge boomer cohort and the trend appears to be accelerating.

FIGURE 2.17

Percent Distribution by Region at Age 25–34

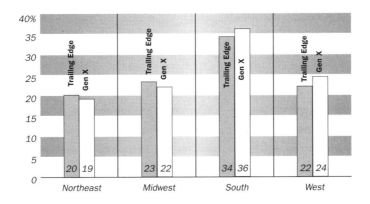

Among the individual states, traditional boomer population dominance is declining as immigration and the longevity of the Post War
generation contribute to larger populations in which the boomers play
a smaller role (*USA Today*, May 29, 2001). Overall, boomers accounted
for 30 percent of the population in 2000 compared with 32.5 percent
in 1990. Higher proportions of boomers today are found in New Eng-
land, among the Rocky Mountain States of Wyoming, Montana, and
Colorado, among the regions of fastest job growth (such as Washington and Oregon) and in some of the expensive Maryland and Virginia
suburbs of Washington D.C.

Cohort Values and Attitude Differences

Little publicly available data compares the lifestyles, values, and attitudes of the cohorts mentioned above at the same ages. Most data on
opinions, values and attitudes has been collected at one point in time,
and identifies differences between cohorts that are different ages. This
masks true cohort differences.

Differences in median household income, for example, are subject
to this kind of misinterpretation. AARP, in its May 2001 *Boomer Brief-
ing Book*, reports on Census data for March 2000 indicating that median
household income for the Leading Edge boomer cohort is $6,000
higher than for Trailing Edge boomers ($61,895 vs. $55,808). However, household income increases with age, so how much of this difference (assuming constant dollars) is the result of life stage and how
much is a difference between the experiences and behaviors of the two
boomer cohorts at the same age? For purposes of the AARP document, this may not be important, but to understand how to adapt marketing programs to successive cohorts in same life stage, this difference
may be very important.

There are, fortunately, some data on behavior and lifestyle differences, which are relatively independent of life-stage influences, although
they are collected at one point in time and compare cohorts at different ages. In these situations, differences in behavior and attitudes
between cohorts can be expected to persist over time and not change
as a cohort moves to a different life stage (ages).

Political and Social Activities of Leading Edge and Trailing Edge boomers

A Roper Starch study commissioned by AARP in 2000, based on a national sample of 2,000 interviews, reports on the percentage of Leading Edge and Trailing Edge boomers engaged in a variety of political and social activities in the past year.

FIGURE 2.18

Participation in Various Activities in Past Year

Leading Edge ☐ vs. Trailing Edge ■ cohorts, in percent

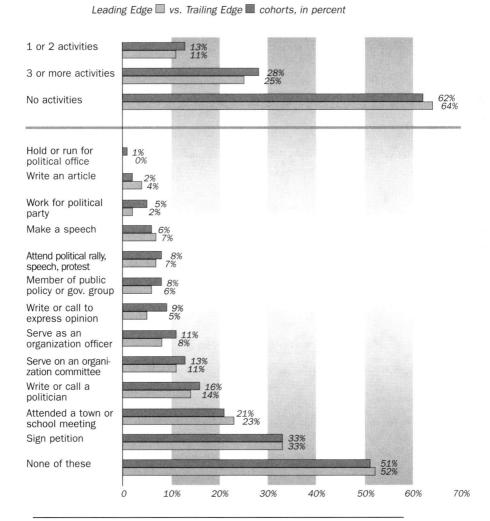

Overall, levels of political and social activities are lower for baby boomers than we would anticipate given the hype about boomer activism. Leading Edge boomers, appear slightly more active than the Trailing Edge boomer cohort, a finding that is consistent with the differences discussed in the literature on the two baby boomer cohorts, but less than the magnitude of those differences as described in the anecdotal literature.

Perhaps the enduring characteristic of baby boomer activism is the reported political and social activity most frequently experienced in the past year—signing a petition. Conversely, 62 percent of the Leading Edge boomer cohort and 64 percent of the Trailing Edge boomer cohort report that they engaged in no political or social activities in the past year.

Attitudes toward Retirement among Leading Edge and Trailing Edge Boomers

AARP conducted an extensive survey of Leading Edge and Trailing Edge boomers in February 1999 using a national random sample survey with a sample size of approximately 2,000 respondents (*Baby Boomers Envision Their Retirement: An AARP Segmentation Analysis*). AARP graciously provided data from this survey for further analysis by cohort. Since this information was collected only at one point in time, we do not have exact "same-age" comparisons. However, the results do provide some insight into cohort differences in areas that are not likely to be impacted by the life stage of the respondent. These are not the ideal longitudinal data, comparing different cohorts at the same life stage (age) to identify specific cohort-based differences.

Views Toward Retirement

Both baby boomer cohorts have relatively positive views of retirement, in keeping with the general perception that this group as a whole is quite optimistic. Although directly comparable data are not available on the Postwar cohort, the general level of optimism is considered a distinguishing feature of this new generation among knowledgeable social researchers at AARP, the leading authorities on the issue. No comparable data are available on the Gen X cohort, so it is not clear if this represents a trend toward more optimistic views on retirement or if this is a view uniquely held by baby boomers.

Leading Edge boomers are slightly more pessimistic in their views of retirement than are Trailing Edge boomers in this survey. This runs somewhat counter to common perceptions of the two cohorts, which holds that the Leading Edge boomers are somewhat more likely to be optimistic and somewhat bullish on the future. The differences, however, are slight, and the overall optimism of both groups of baby boomers is the key finding of this part of the survey.

FIGURE 2.19

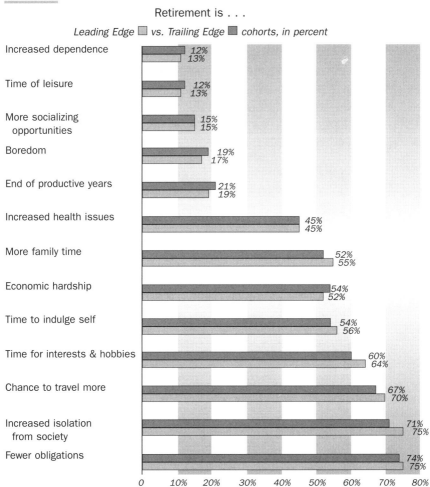

Retirement is . . .

Leading Edge ☐ *vs. Trailing Edge* ■ *cohorts, in percent*

	Leading Edge	Trailing Edge
Increased dependence	12%	13%
Time of leisure	12%	13%
More socializing opportunities	15%	15%
Boredom	19%	17%
End of productive years	21%	19%
Increased health issues	45%	45%
More family time	52%	55%
Economic hardship	54%	52%
Time to indulge self	54%	56%
Time for interests & hobbies	60%	64%
Chance to travel more	67%	70%
Increased isolation from society	71%	75%
Fewer obligations	74%	75%

0   10%   20%   30%   40%   50%   60%   70%   80%

Working During Retirement

Among the survey's most significant insights is the contrast between the expectations of retirement lifestyle of the two baby boomer cohorts, compared with the actual experiences of the Postwar cohort that is entering retirement years.

The retirement lifestyle expectations of the two boomer cohorts are reported in the same AARP survey on retirement. The experience of the Postwar cohort is understood from other AARP surveys on the retirement work status of older (including Postwar cohort) members. It is the overwhelming expectation among both boomer cohorts that they will continue working, at least part time, during their retirement. Generally, however, both boomer cohorts share quite similar views on what they expect of their work life after retirement. This expectation about work is markedly different from the experience of earlier cohorts. This change promises to be one of the most important lifestyle differences affecting those marketing to the Leading Edge and Trailing Edge boomers. The findings on baby boomer expectations about work after retirement, in summary, are:

- Fully eight in ten boomers (84 percent for each cohort) say they plan to work at least part time during their retirement, with only 16 percent of each cohort saying that they will not work at all during retirement.

- Nearly two in five (38 percent of Leading Edge cohort and 37 percent of the Trailing Edge cohort) say they expect to be working part time during retirement, mainly for the sake of interest and enjoyment.

- Approximately one in five (21 percent of Leading Edge boomers and 19 percent of Trailing Edge boomers) say they will work part time during retirement, mainly for the income it provides.

- Others plan to start their own businesses (17 percent Leading Edge and 19 percent Trailing Edge) or plan to retire from their current careers and work full time for pay doing something else (5 percent for Leading Edge and 6 percent for Trailing Edge boomers).

FIGURE 2.20

What I Will Be Doing When I Retire

Leading Edge ▢ *vs. Trailing Edge* ■ *cohorts, in percent*

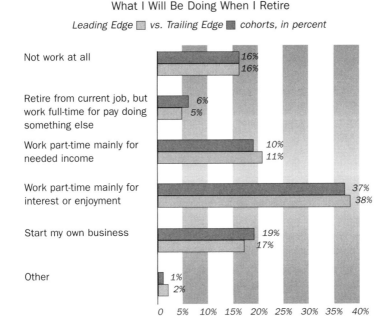

Not work at all — 16% / 16%

Retire from current job, but work full-time for pay doing something else — 6% / 5%

Work part-time mainly for needed income — 10% / 11%

Work part-time mainly for interest or enjoyment — 37% / 38%

Start my own business — 19% / 17%

Other — 1% / 2%

0   5%   10%   15%   20%   25%   30%   35%   40%

Expected Retirement Lifestyles

Responses to several other items in the same AARP Retirement Expectations survey suggest that retirement experiences for both Leading Edge and Trailing Edge boomers will be similar. At the same time, these anticipated retirement lifestyles would be quite different from the experiences of the Postwar cohort. These differences include:

- Only about one-third (32 percent each) expect to move away from the area when they retire;

- More than one-half (57 percent and 56 percent) expect to exercise regularly during retirement;

- Fewer than one-fifth (20 percent and 17 percent) expect to live alone during retirement;

- About one-third (31 percent and 33 percent) expect they will have plenty of money when they retire.

FIGURE 2.21

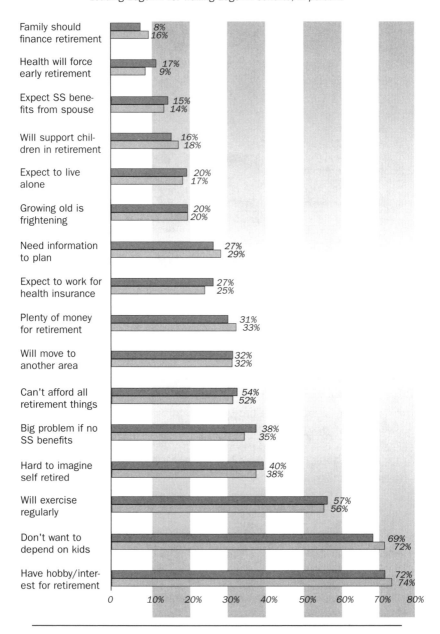

Statements about Retirement that Apply to Me

Leading Edge ☐ *vs. Trailing Edge* ■ *cohorts, in percent*

Family should finance retirement
8%
16%

Health will force early retirement
17%
9%

Expect SS benefits from spouse
15%
14%

Will support children in retirement
16%
18%

Expect to live alone
20%
17%

Growing old is frightening
20%
20%

Need information to plan
27%
29%

Expect to work for health insurance
27%
25%

Plenty of money for retirement
31%
33%

Will move to another area
32%
32%

Can't afford all retirement things
54%
52%

Big problem if no SS benefits
38%
35%

Hard to imagine self retired
40%
38%

Will exercise regularly
57%
56%

Don't want to depend on kids
69%
72%

Have hobby/interest for retirement
72%
74%

0   10%   20%   30%   40%   50%   60%   70%   80%

Summary

- Leading Edge boomers and Trailing Edge boomers are two groups with distinctive experiences, distinctive lifestyles and distinctive behaviors that must be understood to successfully market to them.

- Successful marketers need to take account of how the behaviors and lifestyles of Leading Edge boomer and Trailing Edge boomer cohorts differ from those preceding them, the Postwar cohort, and the following cohort, Gen X.

- Same-age incomes (in constant dollars) are higher for Leading Edge boomers than for members of the postwar cohort. Same age incomes are higher for Trailing Edge boomers than for members of the Leading Edge boomer cohort.

- Leading Edge boomers are more racially and ethnically diverse than were the Postwar cohort. Trailing Edge boomers are more racially and ethnically diverse than the Leading Edge cohort.

- Levels of educational attainment increase significantly from the Postwar to the Leading Edge boomer cohort and slightly from the Leading Edge to the Trailing Edge boomer cohort.

- The proportion of each cohort living in the South and in the West increases slightly with each successive cohort.

- Boomers as a total group are not very politically or socially active, and the differences between activity levels of the Leading Edge boomer and Trailing Edge boomer cohorts are minimal.

- As Leading Edge and Trailing Edge boomers look toward retirement, they are bullish regarding their expected lifestyles and behaviors, and in general, the Trailing Edge boomers are more bullish than the Leading Edge boomers.

- Most baby boomers, both in the Leading Edge cohort and in the Trailing Edge cohort, expect to work after retirement, either full-time or part-time.

- Looking ahead to retirement, the expectations of Leading Edge and Trailing Edge boomers suggest that they will lead much more active and engaged lives than will cohorts who have retired before them.

Special thanks go to Elizabeth Ames, JoAnn Kunberger and Julie Dowse. They have all provided substantial assistance in the collection and analysis of the data reported in this chapter.

3

Current Boomer Behavior and Attitudes: What the Surveys Show

Howard Willens
President, Mature Marketing & Research

The basis for this chapter is three studies conducted by Mature Marketing & Research among national probability samples of baby boomers in October, 2002, March 2002, and November 2001.* These studies focused on what many believe to be "traditional" issues, i.e., issues about which this age group would be most concerned; these include travel, financial planning, and health care. They also incorporate several not-so-traditional issues, like the place of technology in their lives (especially computers), their dining out habits, the vehicles they drive, as well as their cultural activities and attitudes toward life in general.

All data are derived from telephone studies conducted among a national probability sample of baby boomers.

The presentation of findings for each category includes an interpretation of their impact for marketers and advertisers, especially in light of the current stock market and other economic conditions.

What We Learned

Boomers have definite ideas about the world around them They are of this world, in this world—and are very much participants in the political and social life of the country, yet more than half do not participate according to Roper surveys (see p. 31).

They understand that this is a changing world—and they are willing to accept that change. Almost four out of five would consider voting for a woman, or for a Jewish candidate, in the next presidential

Mature Marketing and Research, 232 Cedarhurst Ave., Suite 27B Cedarhurst, NY; 516-569-5904; GenerationG@att.net; and 85 India Row, Suite 30A, Boston, MA 02110; 617-720-4158; mmrharris@aol.com election. The Boomers have definite ideas on what they believe is good for the political life of the country, as shown in the second part of the table below.

FIGURE 3.1

Views of Politics

in percent

	Total	Age 45-49	Age 50-55	Gender Male	Gender Female
Would consider voting for a woman in next Presidential election	77%	77%	77%	72%	81%
Would Consider voting for a Jewish candidate in next Presidential election	79	82	76	76	82
Would vote for Al Gore for President if he ran again	40	44	35	39	41
Believe Presidential candidates should be limited in the amount they can spend on their campaign	77	77	78	77	77
Believe the Federal Government should have a larger role in adopting a national health plan	52	56	48	53	51
(Base)	*(250)*	*(128)*	*(122)*	*(127)*	*(123)*

Survey conducted in March 2002

- Almost four in five believe in spending limits for presidential campaigns
- Forty percent, or two in five would vote for Al Gore if he entered the presidential race again
- One-half believe the country should adopt a national health care system.

Boomers also told us they are taking stock of their past and are beginning to take control over their lives. More than one-half state they are looking forward to the future. Rather than sitting still and contemplating their retirement—or merely planning to do something commonplace when they do retire. This group is ready to begin some big new experience.

FIGURE 3.2
How They Feel About the Future

Strongly/Somewhat Agree (percent)	Total	Male	Female
I have reached a point in my life where I am ready to begin some big new experiences.	46%	48%	44%
In the last few years, I have become much more active about taking control of my finances and my future stability	84	80	88
(Base)	(250)	(127)	(123)

Survey conducted in March 2002

Boomers, whom we also refer to as the mature market, have an interest in what is happening around them, especially when it affects them directly. Thus, they do not hesitate to speak out—either singly or as part of an organized group (e.g., AARP). They began to come of age during the "Age of Aquarius"—so the concepts of activism, liberalism, and change are nothing new to them. Remember their motto: "Don't trust anyone over 30!"

As a further result of their early upbringing, boomers tend to have a strong focus on self. With this background, they have developed definite ideas about what is good for them and for the country. Many have become active in politics and knowledgeable about politics and politicians.

As a further carryover from their past, the boomers are unlike all previous generations facing the age of retirement. That is, they seem to be actually looking forward to this next phase of their lives. They are actively planning for their retirement years by saving, investing, and looking forward to more than just sitting around, playing golf, or travelling.

In many cases they are planning for extra income with new careers as entrepreneurs or teachers. Others, who neither need nor want the extra income, will give of their time as volunteers. The overall attitude of both groups in these instances is to contribute—to give back to a society that for the most part has been very good to them.

Boomers are not waiting for things to happen. They are actively planning for—as well as living—their futures.

In this post-9/11 world:

- Almost all boomers are still at their same job.

- Four out of five (82 percent) indicate they have not changed their retirement plans, and are *actively* planning for their financial future—women to a greater extent than men.

FIGURE 3.3

Perceived Adequacy of Planning

	Total
Have planned well	32%
Have planned some, need more planning	49
Have done little planning	11
Have done no planning	8
(Base)	*(250)*

Survey conducted in March 2002

Four out of five (81 percent) feel they have planned well, or at least have gotten a good start at it.

One in five has done little or no planning.

- Overall, the planning process is most likely to be a joint activity of the male and female heads of the house—when both are present.

Referral, reputation and past performance are key when they choose the assistance of a financial planner:

- *Women lean more towards referral.*

- *Men tend more towards past performance.*

Few (14 percent) subscribe to an investment newsletter—likely reflected in the low percentage (11 percent) involved with trading on the internet.

The maturing market continues to look ahead to its retirement. They are planning for the accumulation of adequate funds (in addition to Social Security) to support a comfortable lifestyle.

For the most part, these people grew up in households where little, if anything, was denied them. The result is that "they want what they want"—and they are now taking the steps to see that they will not be in want when they retire.

Seemingly affected by the events of September 11, 2001 they have become somewhat cautious with regard to their employment and to their investment planning. These cautions have, of course, been magnified by the stock market downturn of 2002. Chances are, therefore, that many either plan to continue their employment longer, or will seek employment and business opportunities for their "retirement."

Therefore, investment houses and planners seeking to attract or maintain a relationship with these boomers need to recognize the new levels of caution—and tailor their services and communications programs accordingly.

Boomers are active participants in their own health care

many boomers are highly concerned with—and are now participating in—their physical well-being (women to a greater extent than men).

FIGURE 3.4

Looking After Their Health

	Total	Male	Female
Try to cut back on specific foods/quantities	55%	56%	54%
Take vitamins and/or mineral supplements	52	40	64
Walk as exercise 3-5 times per week	49	42	56
Have exercise equipment at home and use it	32	34	30
Take herbal supplements	15	10	20
Belong to a health club	13	14	12
Use commercial weight reduction program	10	8	12
None of these	13	14	12
(Base)	(100)	(127)	(123)

Survey conducted in November 2001

- Some are dieting—by cutting back on specific foods and quantities, or by putting themselves onto a commercial weight loss program such Weight Watchers or Jenny Craig.
- Also, some take vitamin and mineral supplements.

- They are exercising by:

    Walking

    Using exercise equipment in their homes

    Belonging to a health club

As they near retirement—and think about their futures—boomers are apparently planning to make those futures last as long as possible. That is, they have decided to begin taking care of their bodies—bodies that in many instances have been neglected over the years.

Not only are they carefully monitoring their food intake, and supplementing that intake with vitamins and minerals, but they are also beginning to exercise long-dormant muscles including the heart, all in the cause of being around to enjoy their retirement and grandchildren.

In so doing, they are opening up new avenues for marketers—not only for foods, supplements and exercise equipment, but also for products and services of all kinds.

Boomers Think and Act Young

Boomers are young-thinking people who are active in the world around them. They are very much a major part of American life—because while they are the "maturing market," they are still a young and vital market (and, a relatively wealthy one at that). They travel, they eat out, they buy cars. They also have some very definite ideas about who they are and what they like with relation to these activities.

They like to travel—and they do so frequently

- Who is traveling?

    Four out of five boomers have taken al least one vacation trip in the past 12 months, and are actively planning another vacation trip in the next 12 months;

    70 percent have taken two or more trips;

    25 percent have take more than four.

- Where are they going?

    Nearly one-half (49 percent) of those planning a trip in the next 12 months have targeted a site in the continental

U.S., while an additional 6 percent have targeted Alaska and Hawaii.

• How are they going?

Most of those with plans (60 percent) will be flying to their destinations.

Delta is their airline of choice, followed by Southwest, American and USAirways.

Another 7 percent are planning a cruise.

The balance (33 percent) are planning to travel by bus, train, RV, or automobile.

When they get to their location, many plan to stay at one of the well known, somewhat lower-priced, hotel or motel chains, including:

Holiday Inn
Best Western
Days Inn (especially those over age 50)
Marriott
Hilton

What it means for marketers

Boomers love to travel. They travel quite frequently on vacation—and by astute financial planning, are seeking to guarantee the means to continue with this activity (as well as any other activities that may strike them).

Likely reflective of post-September-11 thinking, many boomers are planning to take their vacations primarily within the continental U.S. Thus, it would behoove cruise lines to gain an understanding of boomer vacation wants and needs in an effort to boost the low rate of those planning on a cruise vacation.

Travel companies and planners especially can take advantage of the current situation by reassuring potential travelers of the safety features and precautions they have installed, as well as to present unique events, destinations, fares, and packages. They would also do well to take advantage of the boomers' current tendency to focus heavily on vacationing at "home."

They like to eat out—and they do so frequently

At a fast-food restaurant

All have eaten at a fast food restaurant in the previous three months.

More than one-half have had fast food between one and three times per week (men somewhat more than women).

They patronize hamburger chains more than the others with McDonald's and Burger King the most frequently patronized. Men are more likely to eat at Wendy's.

Taco Bell and Pizza Hut are the leading non-hamburger chains among boomers.

A quick, moderately priced meal in a convenient location, with easy parking, are the primary reasons that boomers choose a fast-food restaurant.

Although both male and female boomers patronize fast-food restaurants quite heavily, men have stronger feelings for or attachment to them.

FIGURE 3.5

Fast Food Is a Favorite for Men

Reasons for eating at a fast food restaurant, other than lunch on a workday

Very or Somewhat Important	Total	Male	Female
Like the atmosphere	62%	68%	56%
Feel at ease/comfortable with other patrons	60	68	52
Special food I like	59	66	52
Social event with family	46	46	46
Comfortable, feels like home	46	48	44
Cost is inexpensive	45	50	40
Social event with friends	36	44	28
(Base)	(100)	(50)	(50)

Survey conducted in March 2002

Based upon why fast-food restaurants are patronized at all, they seem to be a "man's kind of place." That is, male boomers, more than female boomers, prefer fast-food restaurants for:

Their atmosphere and the feeling of comfort they provide.

Being a place to relax—either alone or with friends—and be themselves.

Providing a food they specifically like (at the restaurant they frequent most often)—and at an inexpensive price.

Being a place at which they may eat by themselves, should they choose.

Women, more than men, see fast-food restaurants as a place to take their grandchildren.

At a "tablecloth restaurant"

Boomers visit tablecloth restaurants less frequently than they visit fast food restaurants, but tablecloth restaurants do generate more intense feelings about the benefits and features they provide.

FIGURE 3.6

Women Like Tablecloth Restaurants

Reasons for eating in a tablecloth restaurant rather than a fast food restaurant on a workday

Very or Somewhat Important	Total	Male	Female
Like the atmosphere	84%	72%	86%
Feel at ease/comfortable w/other patrons	82	76	88
Special food I like	80	80	80
Social event with family	82	78	86
Comfortable/feels like home	69	66	76
Cost: is inexpensive	70	68	82
Social event with friends	76	74	78
(Base)	*(100)*	*(50)*	*(50)*

Survey conducted in March 2002

Boomers perceive tablecloth restaurants to be more special, and to deliver atmosphere (as well as good service and higher prices). Thus, they are more of a place to observe a real social occasion with spouse, family or friends.

Women have a greater appreciation—and more intense feelings for all these features—than do men.

They own vehicles—generally more than one, and sometimes more than one type

Reflecting a change in both attitudes and likely, some spillover from September 11, one-half of the boomers sampled, both men and women, believe domestic vehicles to be the equal of imports.

Ownership

- 95 percent own one or more vehicles
- Three out of four boomers own two or more
  - *40 percent own three or more*

Of the vehicles owned by boomers:

- *More than 70 percent are of domestic origin*
- *More than one-half are four years old or less.*

FIGURE 3.7

All kinds of Vehicles

Types of vehicles owned	Total	Male	Female
Family Car	62%	56%	68%
Pick-up Truck	33	34	32
SUV	21	28	14
Minivan	16	10	22
Sports Car	9	14	4
Sporty Car	6	6	6
Mid-Luxury Car	6	8	4
Luxury Car	5	6	4
Convertible	1	0	2
No Car	1	2	0
(Base)	*(250)*	*(127)*	*(123)*

Survey conducted in March 2002

"Family car" is by far the term cited most often (62 percent) by boomers as defining or describing at least one of the vehicles they own.

Women are more likely than men to describe their vehicle as family car or minivan.

Men are more likely to name an SUV or sports car as the vehicle they own.

One in three, women as well as men, now own a pickup truck.

Given a choice of vehicles they would most like to own (if they had a choice):

The vast majority named a luxury car—primarily an import:
- Jaguar S-Class
- Mercedes 500 Series (men more than women)
- Lexus 400 & 300
- BMW 535
- Lincoln Continental

SUV, pickup trucks, and minivans followed in that order.

Vehicle choice is related to the following characteristics:

Boomers list dependability, price, and safety as the leading characteristics they seek in a vehicle, at least on the surface.

FIGURE 3.8

Choosing a Vehicle

Reasons for Choice of Vehicle	Total	Male	Female
Dependability	53%	46%	60%
Price	43	42	44
Safety	38	28	48
Quality	29	34	24
Comfort	27	22	32
Economical/good gas mileage	24	20	28
Appearance	21	20	22
Performance	19	20	18
(Base)	*(250)*	*(127)*	*(123)*

Survey conducted in March 2002

Women, more than men, tend to prefer a vehicle that promises comfort and safety, as well as economy.

Men, more than women, tend to choose on the basis of what

they perceive to be a high quality, bigger car—one that gives them lots of "toys" (i.e., new and unusual features).

Both men and women also prize price, appearance, and performance.

FIGURE 3.9

Vehicle as a Reflection of Self

Agree very much/somewhat	Total	Male	Female
The vehicle I drive tells the world who I am and how I feel about myself	35%	24%	46%
I feel that any vehicle I drive must reflect my personality	25	28	22
The vehicle I drive should reflect my position & success in the world	23	18	28
(Base)	(100)	(50)	(50)

Survey conducted in October 2002

One-third of boomers—women significantly more than men—feel the vehicle they drive tells the world who they are and how they feel about themselves. They feel that the vehicle is more than just transportation, that it somehow reflects them.

SUVs, pickup trucks, and minivans have become the vehicle of choice for many reflecting both changing lifestyles and an innovative and recovering U.S. vehicle market, although many dream of that luxurious import. The exception seems to be those boomers in the midst of their mid-life crisis, who want that sports car of their dreams.

Boomers and Technology

Boomers live and shop in the modern world. They are involved with computers, the internet and technology.

There is a great deal of published evidence that younger generations have a tendency to look down their noses at their elders—especially when it comes to acceptance and use of new technology. However, boomers have not merely *accepted* what is new—for the most part they have *embraced* it. Boomers are very much participants in, and comfortable with, the computer age.

Almost all (92 percent) own a computer, according to Census 2000 and three-quarters subscribe to an internet service. This compares extremely favorably with the U.S. population as a whole, and suggests that rather than follow, boomers may lead the way. Overall, 51 percent of U.S. households own one or more computers and 42 percent subscribe to an internet service.

Boomer women are substantially heavier users of the internet than are their male counterparts:

FIGURE 3.10

Hours per Week Online

Hours	Total	Male	Female
0–4	39%	34%	44%
5–9	28	36	21
10–14	11	13	9
15–19	11	17	5
20+	11	0	21

Survey conducted in March 2002

21 percent of women who are internet subscribers are on-line for more than 20 hours per week, while no men indicated that use frequency.

With regard to how boomers use the internet:

- E-mail is its almost universal use (94 percent of all boomers).
- More than two-thirds use it to plan trips.
- Three in five seek health or medical information, on the web—women more than men and the older group more than the younger.
- Boomers also use the internet for shopping, banking, personal record keeping, chat rooms, and trading securities.

More than four in five have made a purchase via the internet. Most have made some sort of travel plan or reservations. Of those who have made an internet purchase, the table below shows what they bought.

FIGURE 3.11

What They Are Buying Online

Items purchased via internet	Total	Male	Female
Airline tickets	36%	43%	29%
Books	36	29	44
Clothing	23	20	27
Computer software	19	20	18
Electronics	20	17	24
Other travel reservations	30	31	29
All other	39	40	38

Survey conducted in October 2002

With regard to other technology:

Three out of four boomers own a cell phone.

One in four have fax machines in their homes.

One in four owns a digital camera.

Boomers are technology-oriented. Further, they apparently outstrip the population in computer ownership and internet membership, strongly suggesting that the thrust of their affinity to technology translates to a convenience orientation. That is, having a computer at home and a cell phone makes their lives easier in many ways.

We know from past studies that in addition to their normal use of the computer as a word processor, a substantial proportion keep their personal financial records in either a dedicated program or in a spreadsheet. This includes their budget, records of their investments, and bank balances.

E-commerce marketers, banking establishments, travel providers, and other retailers would do well to develop information and communications programs relevant to this market. Such actions will help these providers tap into a forward-looking market that is not afraid of new ideas, welcomes change, and has already demonstrated that it is committed to this new medium of shopping and planning.

Boomers, Marketers, and Advertisers

Boomers continue to take marketers and advertisers to task for failing to take the interests of the boomer into account in their efforts to sell products and services.

FIGURE 3.12

Boomers Feel Misunderstood

How well marketers understand my interests for new products

Percent Choosing	Total	Male	Female
Excellent	1%	2%	0%
Very Good	12	12	12
Total Excellent/Very Good	**13**	**14**	**12**
Good	37	38	36
Fair	37	32	42
Poor	13	16	10
Total Fair/Poor	**50**	**48**	**52**
(Base)	*(250)*	*(127)*	*(123)*

Survey conducted in March 2002

How marketers understand Boomer needs when creating advertising and public relations

Percent Choosing	Total	Male	Female
Excellent	4%	6%	2%
Very Good	11	14	8
Excellent/Very Good	**15**	**20**	**10**
Good	40	42	38
Fair	33	22	44
Poor	12	16	8
Fair/Poor	**45**	**38**	**52**
(Base)	*(100)*	*(50)*	*(50)*

Survey conducted in October 2002

Only one in ten (13 percent) boomers believe marketers really understand their needs and interests when it comes to developing new products.

Only 10 percent of boomers feel that marketers really understand what motivates them, or seek to attract their interest with their communications programs.

What it means for marketers

Boomers continue to be a market in search of a seller. They want and need, but in ways that are different from younger and older age cohorts. Accordingly, marketers, advertisers, and their advertising and public relations agencies would be wise to cease ignoring this maturing market and begin to take it more seriously. They need to talk to boomers about their needs, including new and meaningful modifications of existing products and services. They need to develop communications programs that gain the boomers' attention, interest, belief, and action.

For successful communication with boomers, marketers and advertisers need to ask questions such as:

- What are boomers buying, using, and doing now?
- What are their needs for the future?
- How do they differ in these from all other segments?
- What is their relative potential contribution to sales and profits?

In short, boomers need to be shown that marketers and advertisers understand them, understand their product and service wants and needs, and that they are willing to speak to them directly.

Marketers and advertisers can take this vital step by overcoming their obsession with the youth market. For their own long-term prospects, they need to address boomers not only as a current market for their products and services, but also as the wealthiest segment existing today.

With a good fix on the demographics and attitudes of boomers, let's move on to some more specific categories.

4

Baby Boom Travel Emphasizes Adventure and Relaxation

Amy Myers and John Nielson
Colle+McVoy CODE50

The difference between landscape and landscape is small, but there is great difference between the beholders.
—RALPH WALDO EMERSON

Whatever your role in the travel and tourism industry, it is likely you have dreamed of capitalizing on the massive market of travelers aged 50 and older in the United States. The statistics alone are as hypnotic as towering palm trees swaying in tropical trade winds, beckoning us to sunny shores and greater profits.

Consider these facts:

- Travelers aged 50 and older consume 80 percent of all luxury travel—vacations usually costing at least $350 per day.

- They take more trips than their younger cohorts do, averaging three trips per year.

- These travelers stay at their destinations longer, spending an average of 16 days on vacation compared with 11 days for those under age 50.

- They spend more money once they arrive—75 percent more per vacation than those aged 18 to 48.

- Roughly 40 percent of travelers aged 50 and older hold passports, compared with about 17 percent of all Americans.

Colle+McVoy CODE50, 8500 Normandale Lake Boulevard, Suite 2400, Minneapolis, MN 55437; 952-852-7500; www.collemcvoy.com/CODE50

- Americans aged 18 to 48 earn an average of two weeks of paid vacation each year. Those over age 50 have four to six weeks of vacation each year and, once they have retired, have the rest of their lives to travel!

Every day, more than 10,000 Leading Edge baby boomers in the U.S. reach 55 years of age and turn their sights toward traveling. Often, their children are out of the house, the mortgage is paid off, the house is fully furnished and the goal of leaving a large inheritance is not a major concern. The freedom years have arrived at last.

Couple those characteristics with the facts that Americans take about one billion trips within their own country every year and are the world's biggest spenders on travel abroad (U.S.$65 billion in 2000 alone, excluding airfare) and it becomes obvious why global competition is ferocious for 50-plus U.S. travelers.

More than Just Impressive Demos: A Real Passion to Travel

More than the size of the market is impressive. Mature Americans also have a passion for travel, expressed by this mantra: "So many places, so little time. Hey, life is beautiful and it's very short."

As we age, our sense of time is compressed, making the present moment increasingly precious. The more we mature, the more important genuine quality time becomes, compared with the size of our bank account.

Moreover, boomers are searching for new answers. RoperASW has documented the decade of our 50s as the phase during which we experience the most change in our lives. Just a few of the significant events many people face during this time include retirement, major diet changes, caring for aging parents, loss of a parent, the last child moving away from home, adult children moving back home, menopause, becoming a grandparent, and divorce. The list goes on and on, compacted in one of the most challenging decades of our lives.

With so many life changes occurring after age 50, the need to escape the burdens of everyday life, to enjoy a well-deserved break, regenerate, and gain a fresh perspective is greater than ever. Thoreau put it well 150 years ago: "We cannot afford *not* to live in the present . . . the gospel according to this moment."

Experiences Rule

Keith Waldon, spokesman for Virtuoso, a network of independent travel agencies, says, "Today's new currency is unique life experiences." Travel is a unique life experience in and of itself. Moreover, travel is most meaningful in later life, especially *travel with a purpose*.

Since aging boomers spend considerable time looking inward, evaluating their lives in terms of personal fulfillment, they are compelled to embark on a "voyage to the interior," as boomer sociologist Todd Gitlin says. Time spent escaping from day-to-day life is unmatched as a way to recharge and grow.

In his book, *The Force of Character*, James Hillman builds the case that the real reason we age is to develop our character. As Hillman says, "It's in our last years that we confirm and fulfill our character . . . aging becomes a revelation of our body's wisdom." Nowhere do we learn more about ourselves than in traveling the world. Of course, this is a key motivation for travel at any age—consciously or unconsciously. As we gain life perspective, however, the determination to deepen understanding of our lives peaks. According to the African proverb, "Travel teaches us how to see."

OUR OWN TRAVELS WITH MATURE CONSUMERS

For more than a decade, CODE50, the mature market group of Colle+McVoy, has specialized in marketing to consumers aged 50 and older. We stay close to maturity in a number of ways. SAGE,[SM] our panel of mature consumers, regularly visits our offices to help us refine our strategic and creative marketing approaches. SAGEclick[SM] is our online version of SAGE, where participants provide us with quantitative input on our work. You'll come across many of their perspectives throughout this chapter.

Based on this ongoing feedback loop of rich, timely opinions, we've developed a group of principles we call Mature Excitement[SM]—themes proven to more effectively connect with and motivate mature consumers to take the next step with our travel and tourism clients. We'll call out how we've leveraged these themes in our case studies.

Of course, the 78 million Americans who comprise the current age 50-plus U.S. population are an incredibly diverse group. That's why, based on our mature market experience and successful marketing campaigns for clients in the travel and tourism industry such as the Turkish Tourist Office, Minnesota Office of Tourism, and Winnebago Industries, we have created a profile of the most valuable travel and tourism 50-plus target audience. We call them Seasoned Travelers.

Understanding and Targeting Seasoned Travelers

We define Seasoned Travelers as savvy, experienced, well-educated travelers with annual household incomes exceeding $70,000. Seasoned Travelers are often characterized as the leading edge of American baby boomers who are true rule-breakers. Individuality over conformity is a consistent boomer pattern. They've always done things differently and as they get older, they continue to demand products and services that fit their individuality.

In fact, Tourism Intelligence International (TII), a highly respected German tourism consultancy, characterizes the group we call Seasoned Travelers as "Individualists." Individualists are the most informed, knowledgeable, and well traveled of the four types. They have money to spend on vacations, frequently use the internet to research future journeys, are the most resilient in uncertain times, and interestingly, are traditionally among the first to resume regular travel habits after times of crisis.

In short, Seasoned Travelers are nonconformists who want to be highly involved in their vacations, going to great lengths to satisfy all of their curiosities.

The experiences seasoned travelers crave

The World Tourism Office has identified several emerging trends being driven by Seasoned Travelers, including geotourism and increased desire for authentic experiences that include local culture and closeness to nature. In the words of one 55-year-old traveler, "I got tired of taking my grandkids to the beach to build sandcastles, so I took them with me to Panama City to swim with the dolphins."

To successfully reach Seasoned Travelers, the travel and tourism industry must provide them with "a series of memorable events staged to engage . . . in a personal way." This definition comes from authors Joseph Pine II and James Gilmore in *The Experience Economy.* Their premise is that companies must engage consumers on an "emotional, physical, intellectual, or even spiritual level. The result? No two people can have the same experience. Each experience derives from interaction between the staged event and the individual's prior state of mind and being." Considering the personal diversity and complexity of Seasoned Travelers, these are the types of experiences that will appeal to them—"3-D, in-depth experiences," explains Mike Lomax, president of Society Expeditions, an eco-cruise tour operator.

To prove how important such experiences are in later life, look no further than the popularity of Elderhostel, a not-for-profit organization providing educational adventures for adults aged 55 and better. Elderhostel educational adventures offer access to learning programs at universities, national parks, museums, conference centers, and other sites around the world. Each program lasts one to four weeks and is packed with engaging learning adventures, including lectures, discussions, field trips, and other activities.

Elderhostel offers learning for the sheer joy of it, a powerful example of "travel with a purpose." Says one of Elderhostel's satisfied customers, "Elderhostel is my fountain of youth. I am happily involved with activities and learning from morning to night. It's magical."

All this comes with accommodations that range from on-campus residences to well-appointed hotels, from rustic cabins to berths aboard a sailboat. The point is that Elderhostel's success (and the success of many other emerging tour-operator-type companies tapping these same motivations) is based on providing high-quality personal-growth experiences, not catered experiences. Their customers set the bar of expectations for the rest of the travel and tourism industry: "I've seen enough of the world that I don't get too excited about traveling except to Elderhostels," says another customer. In 2000, this formula drew more than 250,000 aging adventurers to 10,000-plus Elderhostel programs in more than 100 countries.

Seasoned Travelers yearn for new, distinctive experiences that deliver meaning, breadth and revitalization. The only players in the travel and tourism industry who will succeed with this market are those who understand how to connect and motivate Seasoned Travelers to visit their destinations, experience their services, or try their products.

The better everyone in your travel and tourism organization understands these core motivations for traveling in later life, the more effectively you can market to Seasoned Travelers and serve them in ways they'll never forget.

Key Segments of Seasoned Travelers

What makes Seasoned Travelers tick? What key messages motivate them? It is only fair to say this audience is constantly moving and shifting, but we have identified and explored five key segments, opening the door to learning how to communicate more intimately with them:

Historical Romantics

Road Warriors

Luxury Seekers

Cultural Explorers

Experiential Adventurers

These segments have emerged from our past work in the travel and tourism industry and surveys conducted with more than 1,000 U.S. Seasoned Travelers.

Let's meet some of the people who represent the five mindset segments of the Seasoned Traveler. While there is some overlap among segments, in general, each type of Seasoned Traveler seeks a specific type of travel experience. The better we understand these segments, the more effectively we can position our travel and tourism products and services as gateways to the experiences each segment seeks. And the more effectively and efficiently we can communicate with "an audience of one" versus trying to sell to the masses.

Historical Romantics

Historical Romantics are well-educated travelers who seek personal connections with the past. They love to
roll up their sleeves and dig deep into
history, both figuratively and literally,
emerging with new discoveries about
their own lives. Historical travel allows
them to connect with themselves and
loved ones on a deeper, more mean-

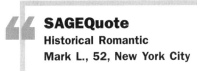

SAGEQuote
Historical Romantic
Mark L., 52, New York City

*History gives meaning to my
life. I love the romance of travel.
I love to do in-depth research
about where I'm going first.*

ingful level. They often already have historical passions such as arche-
ology, photography, architecture, or genealogy, are avid researchers,
and are eager to visit exotic destinations to feed their passions with
challenging experiences.

Historical Romantics tend to be well traveled and are not afraid to
travel to less-developed areas of the world. Not surprisingly, Historical
Romantics have traveled to the Mediterranean more than other segments. There they find abundant ruins and ancient history. Considered
the "birthplace of western civilization" and the "place where East meets
West," it is no wonder Historical Romantics love this area of the world.

Still, Historical Romantics have their limitations. While they are
interested in learning and traveling to unique foreign destinations, they
will not sacrifice comfort and safety to do it. This sounds obvious, but
the risk-reward analysis Historical Romantics conduct is usually quite
different from that of other Seasoned Travelers. Still, the amount of
calculated "travel risk" Historical Romantics will accept is usually unac-
ceptable to other segments.

A Case Study

Through primary and secondary research, we confirmed that Historical Romantics are Turkey's primary U.S. consumer target. Our communications strategy was to achieve familiarity of the unfamiliar through
well-known legendary figures such as Aphrodite, Cleopatra, and Alexander the Great, not with shots of "happy natives," adorable children and
crowds of tourists descending upon Turkey. Ads that engaged every

dimension of this segment in a visceral way were produced, connecting with Historical Romantics in an intellectual, historical and of course, emotional manner.

As a long-haul destination from the United States, Turkey had to offer something unique. To bring this travel opportunity to life for Historical Romantics, we also tapped into our CODE50 themes of Mature Excitement,^{SM} such as Romance, New Experiences and Personal Growth, all natural gateways to the Turkey travel experience.

Turkish Tourist Office Print Campaign: *Targeting Historical Romantics with history and mystery*

But it takes more than just print advertising to draw Historical Romantics to Turkey. To reinforce the travel security message, we leveraged a focused public relations effort, presenting positive, objective stories that illustrated the safety, comfort, and sights available in Turkey. The media strategy included many "special interest" books on the history of the region in an effort to target other passions unique to Historical Romantics, not just their love of travel.

Trade education was another key in increasing travel to Turkey. Strategies included participating in trade shows, providing support materials, and creating a certified agent program, all critical in building knowledge and familiarity for any emerging destination.

We even suggested environmental and structural changes to travel agents' offices, picking up some ideas from our financial industry experience, where we have recommended that advisors remodel their offices to make them more comfortable to their mature clients. The details count too, such as using real coffee mugs (not disposable cups), displaying family photos and accreditations, keeping spare reading glasses on hand, and ensuring guest chairs are comfortable and accessible.

These integrated efforts, blending history and mystery, attracted more than 500,000 U.S. Historical Romantics to Turkey in 2001.

Road Warriors

Road Warriors travel our nation's highways, abandoning the comforts of home for the adventures of the road. These adventures are not without their own amenities, however, often including a motor home equipped with every creature comfort. But Road Warriors don't stop there. Increasing numbers now travel with the latest technology, such as Global Positioning Systems (GPS) and laptop computers linked to the internet so they can send e-mails complete with digital pictures of the vacation in progress to loved ones around the world.

SAGEQuote
Road Warriors
Brenda and Dave F., 61 & 63, Salt Lake City

It's all about independence and freedom on the open road. Sure, we have a plan, but we like to go with the flow, meeting new people along the way, spending time in places we never knew about. Hell, we've got two months out here— why not enjoy all the spontaneity we can?

Road Warriors generally prefer to travel within the United States, visiting sunny spots, national parks, and unique local attractions along the way. This segment includes travelers who are somewhat older Seasoned Travelers and many are retired or work part-time. These folks have a propensity to move throughout the country in tune with small-town happenings. And of course, they love to visit friends and family along the way.

A Case Study

When many Road Warriors set out to see a new or favorite part of the country, they are looking for the type of experience that can only be had from behind the wheel of a recreational vehicle. They want the ultimate in flexibility, the freedom to stop whenever and wherever they want, and the comfort that comes from knowing where they will sleep every night. No company understands those feelings better than Winnebago Industries.

Our most recent print advertising campaign for Winnebago used humor to stress the features Road Warriors prize most: the radio, air conditioning and plenty of accessible storage space for all their must-have traveling equipment. These details may seem trivial to non-Road Warrior types. But behind the wheel of your home-away-from-home, traveling the open road with a very loose itinerary and no hard deadlines, the details heighten enjoyment of the journey.

In addition to humor, other Mature Excitement[SM] themes such as celebrating the present moment and the importance of long-term relationships were emphasized to connect with RV Road Warriors.

As a client for eight years, these marketing efforts have enabled Winnebago to retain its leadership position in the category and helped command a premium price for Winnebago products: a nice position to be in when you consider that Leading Edge boomers are driving the category to new heights, purchasing 1.2 million RVs in the last four years alone, more than in any similar period.

Winnebago Print Campaign: *Featuring creature comforts Road Warriors love*

Luxury Seekers

This segment has a strong desire to be pampered. Luxury Seekers demand personalized service and have high expectations for accommodations and amenities. They are status-oriented and see vacations primarily as time to rest and relax.

SAGEQuote

Luxury Seekers
Jill and Jack S., 51 & 59, Chicago

We expect the best in life and in travel. We don't want to rush on a vacation; we like to relax. Travel should be exotic, romantic and fun, with every detail taken care of for us.

But don't underestimate the value of a unique story to share with their country-club friends upon their return. As the headline in a recent *Cosmos* ad reads, "Tourists bring back trinkets to show. Travelers bring back stories to tell." As well, they like to have names of remote regions to brag about, tales of harrowing adventure, or exquisite pampering to flaunt, and names of legends with whom they've brushed shoulders. These are the stories that maintain their stature among their high-society peers.

Favorite travel experiences include high-end cruises, resorts, fine hotels, and sun-and-sand packages. Since Luxury Seekers crave catered experiences, the more exotic the experience, the better.

This segment has more experience traveling in the Caribbean than do other segments. With that exception, they have not traveled abroad as much as some of the other segments, but they are not opposed to experimenting with new destinations as long as those destinations can deliver the standard of luxury to which they are accustomed.

As evidence of their tendency to look for good service, Luxury Seekers use the internet less than other segments for planning and booking, instead turning to travel agents and other trusted advisors when seeking information and making reservations.

Motivating Luxury Seekers

To successfully target Luxury Seekers, consider following these guidelines at every level of your marketing campaign:

- Present a complete first-class travel experience, providing a sense of how every possible detail is managed.

- Leverage exclusive, prestigious positioning of your product or service.
- Feature unparalleled catered experiences.
- Stress customization, flexibility and personal choice.

Cultural Explorers

SAGEQuote
Cultural Explorer
Wendy D., 49, Minneapolis

I like to go where the locals go, to meet them, experience their lifestyles. My favorite thing to bring back is interesting stories about the people I met and the details of their lives. I love learning about their culture and traditions. Traveling abroad is like a fairy tale, being able to observe and live in a different world than my normal one. My husband likes to explore practically every block of a new city. I prefer to sit on a park bench and talk to someone.

Cultural Explorers are well educated and well traveled, having already visited many areas of the world. Due to their high level of travel experience, they seek unique destinations that are off the beaten path. This segment looks for rich opportunities that will expand their knowledge and cultural experiences. They want to immerse themselves in native culture, experiencing local cuisine and crafts.

For Cultural Explorers, the most rewarding part of any journey is meeting the locals. They not only want to meet the people, they want to make friends with them, live with them, learn from them, even stay in touch with them after returning home. Cultural Explorers have taken the words of Francis Bacon to heart: "If a man be gracious and courteous to strangers, it shows he is a citizen of the world, and that his heart is no island cut off from other lands, but a continent that joins them."

Often seeking destinations with personal significance, Cultural Explorers may be trying to reconnect with their birthplaces, tracing their roots or visiting sites significant in their family history, approaching these opportunities as pilgrimages. They are looking for deep fulfillment and strive to absorb as much as possible of the culture and color of their chosen destination, especially as they relate to these travelers' own personal histories.

This group often will travel great distances and to remote regions for personally significant, once-in-a-lifetime experiences. And several generations may travel together, with older members of a family subsidizing travel of younger family members. Tracing their roots is the ultimate "voyage to the interior."

Cultural Explorers are more adventurous than other segments and are attracted to more areas of the world. They are go-getters in the sense that they don't just want to lie around on vacation or in their lives. This group does not diminish with age, containing more people over age 60 than all other segments.

Cultural Explorers are internet-savvy and like to do their own research about potential destinations. They use travel agents for planning less than other segments, although they may still book reservations with agents. Since Cultural Explorers are "people people," they love spreading the word about their trips once they return home, an important loyalty marketing insight to leverage with this segment.

Motivating Cultural Explorers

Cultural Explorers jump at the chance to get to know new people while on vacation. It's their way of learning more about themselves. This offers a point of emotional connection when marketing to them. They are most motivated with detailed descriptions and rich stories focused on the unique details of local culture. They love to explore other cultural venues and are attracted to outdoor markets, local dance and music performances, and art museums.

Experiential Adventurers

Experiential Adventurers are outdoorsy and prefer more active, adventurous destinations that allow them to be part of an exhilarating experience. This group is leading the trend in soft adventure, seeking out opportunities to hike, bike, swim, kayak, etc. They enjoy opportunities to defy their age and bring back tales of new goals conquered. More educated, experienced, independent,

 SAGEQuote
Experiential Adventurers
Liz and Steve C., 61 & 66,
Los Angeles

Don't tell us what we can't do! We keep ourselves in good shape and love to explore new challenges. We want to push ourselves mentally and physically, but we know our limits. Lying on a beach? Maybe when we get older!

conservation-minded, and respectful of cultures, Experiential Adventurers often travel to more exotic, natural locations and are proponents of geotourism. They're also more likely to be male and self-reliant, preferring to research and book sites themselves, rather than use travel agents.

A Case Study—Marketing Minnesota

In the mature market, more and more people continue to work in later life. The old concept of retirement is dead. Later life really is more like "refirement" as Jim Gamboni has coined it. This is especially true for Experiential Adventurers, who are not inclined to jump into retirement and relaxation. They often continue working until their later years, even working over-time, since they are well advanced in their careers and often have considerable responsibility. That's why Mature Excitement^{SM} themes such as Independence, Creativity and Revitalization resonate so well with Experiential Adventurers.

In the survey we conducted for this chapter and other research we have conducted for our travel and tourism clients, we have found that when these busy people take vacations, they often bring their work with them. Moreover, many don't use all of their available vacation days. What do they need? A replenishing, rejuvenating, refreshing getaway—exactly what Minnesota has to offer, with more shoreline than any other U.S. state.

To really motivate Experiential Adventurers, we had to go further. To most people, replenishment would come from sitting by a lake and reading, but relaxation does not mean the same thing to everyone, and Experiential Adventurers have a hard time sitting still. To target this group, we created a campaign that offered a variety of activities waiting for them in Minnesota, all with a common denominator: water. These images were paired with messages that spoke directly to busy, overworked matures. The ads promote rejuvenation by getting out into nature to bike, hike, swim, golf, kayak, and fish.

Through this campaign, Minnesota became the first state to build a tourism campaign around the needs of the audience. These ads were expanded into a full campaign with outdoor billboards, magazine, radio, and television components, all reminding Experiential Adventurers that vacation time is not to be squandered and Minnesota is the

Minnesota Office of Tourism Print Campaign: *Persuading Experiential Adventurers to make the most of their vacation days*

ideal place to enjoy that time through active vacations in pristine nature. Future targeted tactics include direct marketing partnerships with affinity groups such as AARP. This campaign hit the mark with a 300 percent increase in calls for information on vacation destinations and activities in the first six months of 2002.

Why Target Segments

Naturally, there is overlap among the audience segments one tries to carve out of a mass audience and our Seasoned Traveler segments are no exception. Each segment mindset contains attributes from other segments. But the real value in our segmentation is to reveal the hot buttons of highly motivated mature travelers: what drives their urge to travel, where they look for ideas on destinations, and what types of packages they will purchase for their next vacation. When travel and tourism marketers are armed with these insights, they can more precisely position their own offerings to these segments, build passionate brand campaigns, and follow through with service that heightens a specific experience for each segment.

In this age of differentiation, such targeting is essential. The Seasoned Traveler segments we've outlined will help you accomplish these goals and avoid the traditional, often expensive approach of marketing to all segments at once, which produces hazy, undifferentiated campaigns depicting hazy, undifferentiated destinations.

Opportunities and Challenges for Travel Agents and Destinations

With such propensity to travel, available time and high disposable income, no wonder Seasoned Travelers are so attractive to just about every sector in the travel and tourism industry.

Destinations are attempting to rebuild their tourism revenues after 9/11 and eroding U.S. consumer confidence in 2002. Since fresh, more aggressive, dynamic destinations will be most appealing to Seasoned Travelers, outdated, tired destinations are reinventing themselves, their products and their services to compete for Seasoned Travelers. Established destinations will need to refine how they deliver value and how they differentiate themselves in the minds of Seasoned Travelers. They'll also have to eliminate tourism fatigue as the German tourism consultancy dubs it (that is, workers who are tired of smiling).

On the other hand, emerging destinations need to find innovative ways to stretch their marketing budgets to educate Seasoned Travelers and the travel and tourism industry about the unique qualities and vibrancy of their local cultures. Seasoned Travelers seek authentic experiences. The right positioning against the right segment, executed with the right mix of innovative tactics, is critical to long-term success with Seasoned Travelers among emerging destinations.

The demands are tough. However, the rewards of connecting with such a profitable, resilient, loyal traveler are worth the effort, when you consider that the U.S. population aged 50 to 64 will grow by about 50 percent over the next 15 years.

In the hunt for profitable new clients who can help offset recent commission cuts by airlines and other revenue squeezes, the travel agent sector is working quickly to repackage itself. Travel agents are an important link to the lucrative Seasoned Traveler. Currently, 52 percent of Americans make their leisure travel bookings through travel agents, while more than 90 percent of online travel and tourism sales actually involve retail agents.

Successful travel agent operators will need to develop new travel packages, understanding and getting closer to their best customers, and communicating more intimately with them. Like the other trusted professionals that Seasoned Travelers turn to for guidance (financial advisors, physicians, and attorneys), travel agents can serve the need for credible and trustworthy advice when it comes to planning and booking a new adventure if they can elevate their value and status among Seasoned Travelers. For agents, the following chart outlines why Seasoned Travelers may be their best clients.

Travel Agents' Dream Clients: Seasoned Travelers

Agent Concerns	50+ Solutions
"I'm looking for some serious travelers."	People over age 50 list travel as a top hobby.
"I always feel like I have to down-sell."	Americans aged 50 and older spend over $30 billion a year on vacation travel.
"People come in asking for the cheapest thing even though that's not what they want, then I get blamed when they're disappointed."	50+ travelers are interested in a rich, educational, experiential adventure, and they're willing to pay for it.
"I know it's all in a day's work, but I'm tired only booking super popular, ultra-cheap destinations."	People over age 50 have the time, the money, and the desire to try something new.
"Some travelers get testy when they have to pay my fee. That floors me."	Consumers over age 50 are the most educated age cohort in years. If you respect their knowledge, they'll respect yours.
"I love adventurous travelers—not necessarily physically crazy, but those who aren't afraid of the unknown."	Today, travelers over age 50 are willing to tackle emerging destinations. They don't want the norm. They want a unique, unbeatable experience—a destination that translates into great stories to bring home to their friends and family.
"It's one thing to get them there. Tourism boards also want people to spend while they're there. That's the name of the game."	Travelers over 50 stay longer at a destination and incrementally spend more money than their younger counterparts.

All Seasoned Traveler segments are discerning tourists who place a premium on a seamless travel experience with all the details of their specific type of vacation perfectly in place. As travelers continue to book international trips closer to departure dates to get the best read on local conditions and best available pricing, tour operators realize they need to improve their dynamic packaging abilities, especially by unbundling and repackaging existing tours (often at the point of sale), drawing from multiple inventories, and assigning prices according to predefined rules. Though few have the capability now, operators need to embrace innovative customer relationship management technology for future success.

Cruises and Other Travel Suppliers

Americans take seven million cruises a year, with a large percentage of those enjoyed by Seasoned Travelers. Cruise lines are now consolidating to enhance efficiencies and offer deeper, more consistent value. Since Seasoned Travelers don't want to compromise their lifestyles when they vacation, the major challenge for the cruise line industry is to deliver a top-of-the-line experience that is also cost-efficient. So far, cruise lines are continuing to pay travel agents a booking commission, so they'll need to identify new ways to be as efficient as possible while developing the cruise itself as a unique type of destination.

Beyond cruises, the businesses of many other travel and tourism suppliers are being influenced by the growing numbers and importance of Seasoned Travelers. The key is staying close to Seasoned Travelers to understand the types of travel products and services they seek. Using technology to acquire and retain Most Valuable Customers (MVCs) and Most Growable Customers (MGCs) among Seasoned Travelers is also mandatory. With such insights, suppliers can build key competitive advantages, even new companies that specialize in 50-plus niche markets. A few examples of this approach already exist, including Saga, which owns the Sage Rose, the only cruise ship that caters exclusively to mature travelers. And there's Grandtravel, a tour operator specializing in intergenerational trips (very popular these days, since the average first-time grandparent is just 47 years old). Watch for Silver Sneakers, specializing in walking and snowshoeing tours for folks aged 50 and older. Another player is Back-Roads Travel, which takes groups of fewer than a dozen travelers aged 55 and older on European explorations, using the back roads to discover out-of-the-way places.

Seasoned Traveler Trends: Where They're Headed

An Opinion Research Corporation poll found that about 19 percent of all Americans said they planned to travel abroad in 2002. Compare that to our survey of 50-plus Seasoned Travelers conducted for this chapter, in which 44 percent of Seasoned Travelers reported they plan to travel abroad in the next six months. That's solid proof the drive to travel is alive and well among Seasoned Travelers.

Where do they plan to go?

Our survey revealed these top four regions:

Australia: 88 percent

Caribbean: 87 percent

Western Europe: 86 percent

Mediterranean: 85 percent

What are they looking for?

Collecting new and unique experiences, of course. They want the opportunity to return with the best stories. A few destinations are already going for the jugular with rather extreme offerings:

Netherlands: Frozen Dead-Guys Festival

Ukraine: Tours to Chernobyl

Romania: Dracula Theme Park, scheduled to open in 2003

One of our tourism colleagues, Colleen Lessard, said it well: "When destinations stop trying to be all things to all people, they've taken the first step toward success with a specific traveler looking for a specific experience." Together with our clients and colleagues, we've outlined some emerging destinations believed to have serious future appeal to various Seasoned Travelers segments just described.

Scandinavia is not "first tier." However, given the relatively strong concentration of Scandinavian ancestry in specific U.S. markets, and the growing interest in tracing or connecting to one's family roots, Scandinavian destinations stand to do well with future Seasoned Travelers, especially the "re-connectors" among Cultural Explorers.

Iceland is being used as a new gateway to European hubs, giving it a much-needed boost in awareness. Once its unique culture and wide variety of natural wonders are promoted, Seasoned Travelers (especially Experiential Adventurers) will flock there.

Southeast Asia These are long-haul destinations that appeal to travelers with time for extended-stay vacations, above-average income, a strong desire to learn about different cultures, and a sense of adventure. Take Vietnam, for instance, a destination that is overbuilt for a U.S. tourism boom yet to materialize. Or Cambodia, with its incredible display of ruins at Angkor Wat, which is poised to benefit from the Seasoned Travelers' desire to explore natural wonders and experience different cultures.

Costa Rica is a good example of a destination in the Caribbean that is not pure "fun-in-the-sun." Costa Rica appeals to Seasoned Travelers because of its diversity of natural wonders and ecology. Its well-developed infrastructure and good proximity to the United States make Costa Rica a desirable, affordable, safe destination for those interested in a wide variety of soft adventure and ecological and natural wonders without sacrificing beautiful Caribbean beaches.

Brazil has only recently begun to target U.S. Seasoned Travelers. In the past, most of its tourism efforts were concentrated on the areas of Rio and Sao Paulo, where beaches and shopping were the main attractions. Now, however, Brazil is poised to capitalize on the trend of exploring destinations rich in culture, natural wonders, and ecological diversity—all strong attributes of the other, less well-known areas of Brazil. Major U.S. airlines have placed new emphasis on their South American routes that in the past were plagued by load factors that were heavily skewed in favor of northbound travel.

The truth of the matter is that many Americans are deficient in their knowledge of world history and geography. However, Seasoned Travelers are different. They're committed to lifelong learning. And, once educated on unique regions of the world, they'll descend upon destinations in search of new experiences that will help them better understand their place in the world.

Up for the challenge?

Imagine delivering this "dream vacation" as requested by one of our SAGE members:

> *Take the Concorde to Paris and then the bullet train to the south of France. Use multidimensional travel between high-end dining and lodging facilities by hot-air balloon and bicycle. Take the bullet train back to Paris and then the Chunnel to London where we take a limo to the QE2's docking facilities to embark on an around-the-world trip back to San Francisco. Stay overnight at the Stamford Court or Ritz Carlton and then return via helicopter to Sacramento after a wonderful dining experience at Kuleto's on Powell St. Luggage to follow.*

Get a good sense of the rhythm of this dream vacation. More often, Seasoned Travelers will demand a new mix of planned/spontaneous, active/reflective, and authentic/luxurious travel experience.

Build A Marketing Journey for the Seasoned Traveler

Unlike most product and service offerings, travel is unique in that the phases of anticipation and recollection can be as important, or even more important, than the actual product experience. The more defined your Seasoned Traveler target the more effectively you can leverage the anticipation and recollection phases. This is the essence of successful relationship marketing in the travel and tourism industry, where market intelligence, innovation, and closeness to customers are the new imperatives.

Marketing Touch Points during the Consumer Journey

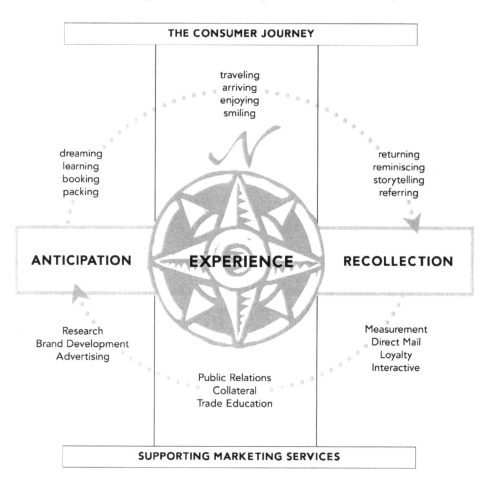

The right marketing approach will intimately surround Seasoned Travelers in every one of these phases for, as Francis Bacon reminds us, "When a traveler returneth home, let him not leave the countries where he hath traveled altogether behind."

5

Boomers on Drugs: Marketing Healthcare Products to the Baby Boom Generation

Anne Devereux
President, BBDO Health

The Baby Boom Generation has formally entered middle age. Or has it?

For past generations, the term "middle age" conjured up images of graying hair, slowing bodies, sedentary activities, and the beginning of a health decline. Bob Hope said that, "Middle age is when your age starts to show around your middle."

However, what middle age means to boomers—in terms of self-perceptions, behavior, needs, and demands—is often quite different than our parents' definition. It is often defined by how we're "feeling." It is defined by our "health."

That is because we're not our parents' version of middle aged. We feel young, vibrant and vital unless health issues force us to think otherwise. Moreover, when health issues do arise, we want to address them immediately so that we can go back to feeling as young as we see ourselves.

A study by the MacArthur Foundation confirmed that health issues create a gap between how old we *are* and how old we *feel*. Their study, which interviewed thousands of boomers, found that boomers actually see themselves as five to fifteen years younger than they really are. In fact, people aged 45 to 54 feel like they are 41, and people aged 55 to 64 feel 48.[1]

BBDO Health Work, 1285 Avenue of the Americas, New York, NY 10019; 212-459-6240; Anne.Devereux@bbdo.com

So, what happens when there is a gap between the age of our bodies and the age at which we see ourselves? There is evidence that shows boomers share a number of common experiences and behaviors relating to their bodies and their health:

- Boomers hate it when "reality"—the aging process—reveals their age. They struggle to preserve the appearance of youth, looking for miracle diets, wrinkle-reducing creams and electric pulse exercise belts that offer the perception of fitness without the actual effort.

- Boomers also hate it when they realize that they are no longer physically able to do what they could do. When they choose to exercise, they frequently push themselves too far and suffer from the resulting sports injuries or "morning after" pain and stiffness.

These issues—feeling young, yet noticing physical limitations, looking for ways to restore feelings of youth, and being forced to address the reality of the aging process—will be addressed in this chapter.

The Definition of Health

For our parents' generation, health meant "the absence of disease." If they did not have cancer or weren't suffering from chronic pain, they saw themselves as healthy. Moreover, their expectation of the doctor was that he would treat the illness and address the problem with medicine that was safe.

However, for boomers, health means much more. Health not only includes physical well being, but mental health as well. It is inward-focused, as well as externally focused. Science has proven repeatedly that healthy relationships—with family, friends, and even with pets—contribute directly to improved health and extended life. Good health is dependent on addressing all of these life facets.

Physicians today are more than aware of the relationship between life-stress and overall health. That's why when assessing a problem or giving a general physical exam, doctors often ask about how we're doing emotionally. They ask about our marriages and relationships, our jobs, and our children.

Just as the definition of health has extended beyond the "body," boomers think of health from a longer-term perspective as well. Families with histories of chronic, life-threatening diseases like cardiovascular illness and diabetes measure their health against their family history of illness, rather than against the norm or according to their recent doctor's visit. They qualify their good bill of health with, "I'm healthy now, but I have to keep an eye on my cholesterol. My father died at 55."

Boomers' "hippie" experiences have also allowed them to be more accepting of the concept of a mind-body connection than past generations. Moreover, if thinking positively can positively affect health outcomes, boomers will be on board. For example, think of the gastrointestinal product category. Research shows that the placebo effect for antacids is near 70 percent. In other words, more than two-thirds of consumers taking a sugar pill to treat their heartburn report that they are feeling better—that the "medicine" worked. The reality is that by thinking they were addressing the problem, their minds actually controlled either the production of acid or the sensitivity of the esophagus in detecting it.

Health Priorities

Because of this broadening definition of health and the character traits that tend to be common among boomers, our priorities for healthcare have changed.

Yankelovich, a world-renown research firm that has been following the behavior of boomers for the past twenty years, reports that boomers' health priorities differ dramatically from past generations. Boomers have high expectations for treatment and low acceptance of failure. They have rebelled against authority, valued freedom and access to information, and now live at a time where advanced medicine allows people to live through life-threatening events that would have killed them a decade before. With access to information, they don't see doctors as the ultimate authority. They understand that medicine—treating illness—is art as much as it is science. Moreover, along with the art, they're looking for magic.

They do not have patience for drugs that take two weeks to work, like those prescribed for depression, or for medicine that works without making them "feel any better" or "notice any positive change." Immediate results are a priority.

Great expectations

Boomers expect to feel better quickly, experience the improvement, and feel better about themselves as a result. One without the other (symptom relief without experiencing the end [emotional] benefit) often leaves boomers dissatisfied with the treatment.

In fact, it has become imperative for successful communications or advertising campaigns to help close the mind-body gap for consumers. If products relieve symptoms without making the consumer feel better on a higher emotional level, the communication often is ignored.

Consider the recent campaign launched for the antidepressant, Zoloft. The campaign is executed in black and white cartoon-like style, with a deflated ball representing a person suffering from depression. After taking Zoloft, the ball-person is portrayed as "fully inflated," smiling, and bouncing off into the future. It is a typical problem-solution execution. Right?

Wrong. Cleverly, the brand and agency team executing the advertising understood an important boomer insight. Many boomers avoid getting treated for depression because they feel responsible, embarrassed, weak, or that their depression is a sign that they have failed in some way. However, in the middle of the problem-solution scenario, the ad campaign uses a simplified visual demonstration to show how depression happens—that it is a chemical process caused by an imbalance of serotonin in the brain. Moreover, serotonin is something that a consumer could not possibly control. So the blame is gone, the stigma is (or should be) reduced, and the result for patients is that not only are they more able to go and get treatment, but their self-image is improved as well. The advertisement addresses the emotional end-benefit. Now, given boomers' demand for instant healing, the brand team needs to support this campaign with educational materials to set appropriate expectations and relationship-marketing programs which get patients to persist with their medicine despite their initial disappointments.

Another example of health advertising that understands the emotional drivers of boomers is an advertising campaign developed by

Merkley Newman Harty for Pharmacia's HRT therapy (Activella). In this ad, the marketers emphasize that the drug not only reduces the symptoms of menopause, but that women can still feel romantic, beautiful, and sexy while going through it. The insight used as a foundation for this campaign was that going through menopause makes many women feel old, uncomfortable, and less desirable, and those negative self-perceptions are as big a problem as the menopause symptoms themselves.

Executionally, this campaign was very aspirational for boomers. The woman used in the ad looks young, beautiful, hip, and vibrant—possessing many of the qualities to which boomer women aspire. The color palette is hip and vibrant as well. Bright orange and green reinforce the contemporary nature of the target customer and the contemporary nature of this brand.

Surprising Behavior

The two campaigns featured above clearly point to prescription product marketers' attempts to reach boomers on intellectual and emotional levels. Still, in both of the categories (depression and menopause) there is considerable resistance to taking drugs. Boomers often feel they should try to fight their problems with "natural" solutions first. For some, that is herbal supplements. For others, it is diet and exercise. In fact, *Prevention* magazine reported that 94 percent of boomers self-treat before seeing a doctor.[2]

However, there's a strange disconnect between this movement towards self-treatment and actual improvements in boomer health and fitness. For example, there are huge increases in the number of boomers joining gyms. Americans over age 55 (Leading Edge boomers) are the fastest growing segment of health club members.

Boomer activities are shifting from sedentary to more active. An article in *American Demographics* (April 2002) about more-active grandparents noted that two to three times more people in this age group were engaging in such activities as weightlifting, playing basketball, and playing videogames than were choosing these activities in 1988. Those participating in backpacking and hiking and aerobic exercise were up more than 100 percent. The number of people in the age group engaged in activities such as playing cards, refinishing furniture, and going on a picnic increased only slightly during the same period. Data were from Mediamark Research, Inc.

Here's the contradiction: Boomers appear to be more active, but the incidence of obesity (and of related conditions like hypertension, diabetes and high cholesterol) has increased exponentially. The National Institute of Health reports that the national incidence of obesity increased by more than 50 percent between 1960 and today. The greatest increase happened between 1990 and 2000.[3] The American Council on Exercise reports that 25 percent of adults never exercise and 60 percent do not exercise on a regular basis.[4] And where there is a constant trend of short-term participation in weight-loss programs, changing behaviors is an uphill battle. Boomers are well familiar with the "yo-yo diet" and the gap between "should and want."

This is the essence of the boomer dilemma: They want to be healthy, but not if they have to work too hard at it.

Just ask someone diagnosed with Type II diabetes. Upon first diagnosis, people with Type II diabetes are generally told by their physician to exercise, to lose weight, and to reduce the sugar and carbohydrates in their diets. For the majority of patients with this disease, compliance with those steps should keep the disease from progressing and reduce or even eliminate the need for medication.

But, despite the potential to quash the disease, two-thirds of patients agree that "following my doctor's recommendations for diabetes care is not easy," and 40 percent openly admit that they "do not feel successful managing their diabetes."[5] Even these admissions are overstated. We estimate that less than one in ten actually follows the recommended diet and exercise regimen.

In fact, one of our clients (who manufactures one of the most prescribed diabetes pills in the world) estimates that fewer than one-third of patients who are prescribed the pill are still taking it one year later. Even fewer of them have modified their diet and exercise regimen in any significant way. Consequently their disease progresses, and uncontrolled high blood sugar results in blindness, amputations of limbs, and even premature death.

While this process of denying the realities of a serious disease is not exclusive to boomers, the behavioral gap is widening as a result of common boomer traits:

- "Searching for the silver bullet"—medicine that will control illness without requiring that we make behavioral changes.

- Denying that diseases will progress to a more dangerous phase, and waiting to take charge until the symptoms are too taxing.

- Feeling comfortable "enjoying the moment" rather than preparing for the future. Boomers are not called the "me" generation for nothing!

Boomers want to stay young and healthy, but in this era of advanced medicine, advanced technology and instant gratification, they are generally not willing to pay the price to get there.

Other contributing factors

While the gap between health risks and the recommended behavioral changes are huge, other environmental factors contribute to this behavior. The advancement of medicine has resulted in a decreased urgency to change behavior. The chart below shows that the risk of death caused by a heart attack has decreased consistently between 1980 and today:

FIGURE 5.1

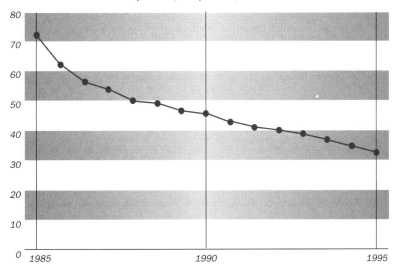

Deaths from Heart Attack Among Ages 45–54

Deaths per 100,000 persons, 1984–1998

Source: National Center for Health Statistics, Data Warehouse on Trends in Health and Aging, www.cdc.gov, May 2003.

Because of the advances in medicine, even the threat of high cholesterol or hypertension leading to a heart attack is less scary than it
used to be. Most boomers know people who have suffered heart attacks
and are still living comfortably so it is easier to put off diet and exercise until tomorrow and have that extra piece of cake.

Broadening the definition of health

Just as we now think of health as more than just the absence of illness,
healthcare is now defined more broadly than the dispensation of pre-
scriptions.

The growth of new categories of care—like "cosmaceuticals" and
"nutraceuticals" broadens the definition of healthcare to include pre-
ventative medicine and facilitates the focus on nontraditional signs of
health (beauty) as well as traditional ones.

Cosmaceuticals include many health and beauty products created
for purposes such as "reducing signs of aging," "rebuilding cartilage,"
and "improving stamina." Both the availability and the use of these
products have increased exponentially over the years. The Fredonia
Group (May 2001) estimates that cosmaceuticals are a $3 billion indus-
try, with demand for these products expected to grow 7.6 percent
yearly to $4.3 billion in 2005.

Further, boomers are resorting to surgery in order to put forward
the face of youth. It is estimated that there are 1.2 million cosmetic,
age-lowering medical procedures conducted each year, with the majority of those being performed on boomers. This is a 198 percent increase
from 1992.[6] Botox use (wrinkle-reducing injections) has grown substantially, making it a $309.5 million brand.

Nutraceutical use (nutritional supplements and vitamins used to
preserve and/or improve health) is even broader. In an annual study
conducted by *Prevention* (the 2000/2001 International Survey on
Wellness), it is reported that 151 million consumers use some sort of
dietary supplement and 106 million take vitamins and minerals daily.
Those numbers include 55 percent of consumers aged 36 to 54 who
take supplements, and 63 percent of people aged 46 to 54 taking vitamins and minerals. With the exception of a couple of key categories,
there is limited evidence or clinical data to support the efficacy of these
supplements. However, in agency focus groups, boomers acknowl-
edged that they are taking them based on faith and the hope that they

will in some way fortify or restore their youth, protect them for the future, or make up for their admittedly poor eating habits.

Freedom and Control

Boomers look for improvements in health options on a consistent basis. Unfortunately, as their search for improved options has intensified, the environment for receiving optimal care within the doctor's office has constricted.

Welcome to the world of managed care

Within the managed-care system, private health insurers have significant influence over how doctors practice and which medicines they prescribe. Formulary policies often require physicians to start patients on an over-the-counter (OTC) product that they pay for themselves before moving onto a prescription brand, and then limit the number of approved medicines available to patients within each health category.

Doctors are given incentives to increase the number of patients they see and to keep a cap on the cost of treating each patient. Consequently, they have less time to spend with patients, fewer treatment options available to them, as well as less time to answer questions about medications and address secondary concerns.

The conflict

With more restrictions on care and more available treatment options, boomers have tremendous incentives to take health into their own hands.

And they're doing just that. As mentioned earlier, *Prevention* magazine reports that 94 percent of Americans are likely to self-treat before seeing a physician, and *American Family Physician* magazine reports that nonprescription medication now accounts for over 60 percent of all medicine used in the United States.

Technology

The technology boom and the subsequent easy access we have to available information fuels the trend to self-care. *Prevention*'s survey reports that nearly 32 million consumers go online for information about prescription medicines. Further, while we think that young people dominate computers and the internet, more boomers (and seniors) are accessing online health information. In fact, *Cyberdialogue* reports that over one-half of the time people search the web, it is for health-related information.

Think about what happens in the doctor/patient relationship because of this access. Patients have hours to spend searching online for information related to their illness. They access pharmaceutical manufacturers' sites, read technical papers published for/by researchers and thought-leaders, access sites put up by other patients, learn the perspective of nontraditional thinkers, and even access the sites of self-proclaimed experts with no real medical training. They compile all of that information and bring it to the doctor who has ten minutes to evaluate and counsel them while keeping costs down. The doctor certainly has not had the time to surf the internet to get all of the information with which the patient comes equipped. The result is further strain put on the already tenuous doctor/patient relationship and increasing confusion and frustration among boomers.

Direct-to-consumer advertising

Over-the-counter products and the internet have definitely increased boomers' ability to access information. In parallel with those developments has been the aggressive move by prescription brands to approach consumers directly about their drugs. Called "direct to consumer advertising," or DTC, marketers use print, TV, and billboard advertising to reach out to their target audience. It is estimated that in 2000, manufacturers spent over $2 billion dollars in this venue.

The strategy seems to be working. *Prevention* reports that in 2000, 91 percent of the nation's consumers had seen DTC advertising. Of those who saw ads, 32 percent talked to their doctor about it, 26 percent asked for specific medicines they had seen, and seven out of ten walked out of the doctor's office with a prescription for that drug.[7]

Health Fears

The media affects health behaviors in other ways, too. Well-organized efforts by the breast cancer community have brought the risk of breast cancer to a top-of-mind awareness among women, making it their number one health fear. However, with the possibility of death as a result of a heart attack five times greater than the risk of death from breast cancer,[8] the media has possibly done boomers a disservice. Bringing breast cancer fears to the forefront, the media may have skewed the focus and reduced the likelihood that women will heed their doctors' advice about lifestyle changes related to less scary but more deadly chronic diseases.

Managed care has introduced new fears as well. Boomers within the United States remember the days of a private health system where they knew their doctors well, could chose to see the ones they wanted, whether generalist or specialist, and could trust the doctor to prescribe the best possible medicine regardless of cost. Now, with the need for referrals from generalist doctors before seeing a specialist, and the restrictions managed care puts on the brands of medicine that can be prescribed, boomers fear they are not getting the best possible care and they are frustrated with the system.

DTC advertising, while bringing information to the public, also provides the public with an increased awareness of the risks and side effects of medicines. Since almost no medicine is perfectly "clean," current FDA regulations require that there is "fair balance" of risks and benefits. Therefore, patients understand that the medicines pose potential health risks as well, and they worry about the ramifications of taking medicine long term. In the past, the doctor did most of the worrying.

How do boomers reconcile the gap between the risk to their hearts if they don't take their medicines with their fear that they could damage their livers if they take medicine indefinitely?

Boomers now carry the burden of increased knowledge. Many carry that burden well, but there is also the risk that boomers will begin to make incorrect assumptions about their care. One unfortunate trend is that many boomers believe (given the average life expectancy of almost 80 years) starting medicine too early might result in wearing out the medicine's effectiveness over time. "I worry that I won't have anything left to try when my illness gets really bad," said an arthritis sufferer we talked to recently. It's an incorrect assumption, but a very common one, and it leads to inadequate treatment and, at times, dangerous avoidance of medicine.

Implications for Marketers

We've talked about many factors that effect boomers' experiences with healthcare:

- The broadened definition of health and increased expectations for treatment,

- The rise and power of managed care organizations,

- Increased pressure on doctors to see more patients and cut treatment costs,

- The rekindled fire of boomer (patient) activism,

- The introduction of direct-to-consumer advertising,

- The age of technology, and

- An emergence of self-care.

For marketers, these trends represent opportunities to reach this influential boomer target, and suggest which type of messages, programs, and products are likely to have appeal.

Messages

Differentiate

From a messaging standpoint, we have to get past the current DTC formula: "product indication" (i.e., pain relief) executed by showing the "end benefit" (i.e., so you can do the things that you like to do). This formula is used in more than half of DTC advertisements today. It does not differentiate. It is not unique. It fails to get at a core insight that truly motivates action and gets to the heart of boomers. Whether the messages are revitalizing, intelligent, complimentary or humorous, boomers need to be reached at a deeper level than product benefit.

Reward Success

As noted throughout this chapter, getting patients to stay on therapy for the long-term is as hard as getting them to accept that they have an illness in the first place. The rise and sophistication of relationship marketing will allow manufacturers to build relationships with patients and families. Over time, making boomer "members" feel part of a greater unit, and rewarding them for their success will have a huge effect on the bottom line. It will serve to facilitate the continuation of revenue and allow marketers to protect their franchise from new entrants and, most importantly, help boomers live longer, healthier lives.

Network, Create Viral Marketing, Develop Communities

Remember the 1960s phrase, "never trust anyone over thirty?" Boomers are used to uniting as a group and sharing strength, information, and opinions with each other. Healthcare marketers who learn how to tap into this viral community will see their marketing dollars have exponential impact as boomers spread the word about the products and services that are helping them live and feel the way they want to.

Choose Celebrities Carefully

Boomers identify with some "stars," but at least an equal number will inspire the opposite reaction.

Honest use of celebrities can be highly effective. One great example is the spot created to encourage smoking cessation featuring Christy Turlington. She quit smoking following her father's death from lung cancer. Glamorous, yet personal, heartfelt, true, and honestly communicated, her message hit at the emotional heart of the issue and resonated with boomers who are now experiencing the death of a parent and desperately want to be around for their own children and grandchildren.

Contrast this with the recent ad campaign for Avandia, a medicine for Type II diabetes. The TV spot features thin, beautiful (and Caucasian) Jane Seymour, despite the fact that she does not have diabetes. Her grandmother had the disease, and the majority of (Type II) diabetes sufferers are overweight, of lower income and educational levels, and skew to minority populations. She was far less appropriate and motivating than Christy.

Programs and tools

The tools needed by boomers are obvious. Intelligent information in easy-to-access places. They don't want to work too hard to find what they're looking for.

Boomers need incentives to keep going and rewards when they do. Memberships in "loyalty" programs—the health-version of frequent flier miles—are great. So are connections to communities that might generally be underground. Bob Dole helped the Viagra marketing team make erectile dysfunction (ED) a common and treatable illness. With Activella, we created a network of women, supporting each other through menopause. In addition, clients of ours launching a product in the field of mental illness are creating a network for friends and family involved in managing the disease.

Products

Over the next fifteen years, the opportunity to introduce products that reach boomers could reap enormous rewards. The largest population segment with the greatest disposable income and the most time to investigate new offerings, boomers are "ripe for the picking." Breakthrough medicine, whether more efficacious than previous options or with safer side-effect profiles will surely be attractive. Devices and courses which help "re-capture youth" without requiring too much exertion are likely to be popular, too. Just look at the growth in yoga, Pilates, and meditation.

The other big opportunity is in nutritional foods. Whether it is products like Viactive, a great-tasting snack fortified with vitamins for women, or the new results of clinical testing that allow Quaker Oats to promote the heart-health benefits of oatmeal, it's a lot easier for boomers to eat something healthy than change life behaviors.

The Most Consistent Mistakes

Our agency is a fairly typical communications company. Our employees are young. The average age of an art director is twenty-seven. Ask a 27-year-old what a 50-year-old looks like, and you're likely to see photos of an old guy fishing or a retired woman gardening. An ad for Pravachol for example suggests grandfather-grandson, sedentary activities, a goal of just staying alive. It is a campaign likely to be dismissed by boomers as "not me."

Boomers do not see themselves as the fishing or gardening set, even if they enjoy those activities. They see themselves as physically active and energetic. Age 35 or 40, max. Relatively youthful. Possibly even glamorous. Not perfect, but close. When we use this understanding in creative executions, wonderful things happen.

The recent Lipitor-campaign TV spot shows the near-perfect boomer. Thin, beautiful and seemingly perfect. She *is* nearly perfect—but her cholesterol isn't. Moreover, since she looks like she does all the right things (diet and exercise) and still has high cholesterol, she's appealing in beauty—and in communicating the message that nobody is perfect, despite the fact that they try to be. That makes having high cholesterol a little more acceptable, and the campaign, much more effective.

The Future

While the future holds great promise for boomers as it relates to health-care and self-care, as marketers we can take one more step.

Finding ways to bridge the gap between patients and doctors will undoubtedly improve diagnoses, treatment, and compliance. Health marketers who recognize that the educated boomer is far more likely to start and comply with therapy will undoubtedly have more success than those who hold back on information.

Moreover, those of us who define or paint the picture of "old age" need to get out a new set of paints. People we have talked to define old age as 90-plus. We boomers have a long way to go.

Notes

1. MacArthur Foundation Research Network on Successful Midlife Development.
2. "International Survey on Wellness and Consumer Reaction to OTC Advertising of Rx Drugs," *Prevention* Magazine
3. NIDDK (Weight Control Information Network); National Institute of Health website www.niddk.nih.gov/heqalth/nutrit/pubs/ statobes.htm#research
4. American Council on Exercise website http://acefitness.org/aboutace/ index.cfm
5. *Doctor's Guide, Personal Edition.* Doctor's Guide Publishing Limited; 1995 (www.pslgroup.com)

6. American Society of Plastic Surgeons; 2000 Cosmetic Surgery Trends www.plasticsurgery.org

7. "International Survey on Wellness and Consumer Reaction to OTC Advertising of Rx Drugs," *Prevention* Magazine

8. Women's Health Hotline; National Women's Heart Health Day Statistics (www.libov.com/nwhd/statistics.html)

6

Baby Boomers and the Fast Food Industry

Ron Paul and Jacqueline Rodriguez
Technomic, Inc.

Thirty-five years ago, as the first baby boomers were coming of age, a fledgling restaurant chain named McDonald's introduced a sandwich called the Big Mac. The timing was portentous for both. Within a few years, the hamburger company was decorating its signs with the slogan "millions served," followed soon by "billions." Other chains followed, offering fried chicken, pizza, and ice cream. These foods soon would become a mainstay for the new parents, divorcees, and upwardly mobile workaholics who were spending less time in the kitchen than their parents ever did.

Perhaps no other American generation is more closely attuned to an American industry. They are two phenomena that have come of age side-by-side, each influencing and responding to the other over the course of three decades. In many ways, the foodservice industry—particularly fast food—provides a reflection of the boomer generation's values and lifestyle. When they clicked, business was great. When tastes changed, sales started to sag. If history is any indication, fast-food restaurants are poised again to shift their focus to this demographic gorilla, offering fresh tastes to a generation ready to retire, but not slow down.

That the fast-food industry has relied for much of its history on baby boomers should come as no surprise. Most consumer products, from running shoes to VCRs, have done the same. Today's all-in-one

Ron Paul is president of Technomic, Inc., 300 South Riverside Plaza, Suite 1940 South, Chicago, IL 60606; 312-876-0004; www.technomic.com. At the time this chapter was written, Jacqueline Rodriguez was a senior consultant.

supermarket was created during this period, evolving from the old neighborhood groceries, fruit markets, and dairy delivery routes. Convenience foods, ranging from the first TV dinners to the trend of so-called "home-meal replacement," also emerged to tap the boomers' need for sustenance. With 76 million boomers looking to eat three times a day, it was inevitable that entire food-related industries would spring up to meet the need.

Even more than other businesses, quick-service restaurants have thrived with boomers as their essential market. Families are a prime market for quick service, so boomers as both children and parents have been crucial to the industry's growth. Currently, children of boomers— Generations X and Y—are the heaviest users of fast food. Boomer women were the first to enter the workplace en masse, consequently, preparing and eating fewer meals at home. Finally, boomers began to make more money than any generation before them and they indulged in a wider range of interests. With disposable income on the rise and free time declining, cooking from scratch became less appealing. During the inflation of the 1970s and early 1980s, however, full-service restaurants remained a luxury for many. Fast food offered an attractive compromise of value and convenience.

FIGURE 6-1

Fast Food Nation

meals served in millions, 1975–2003

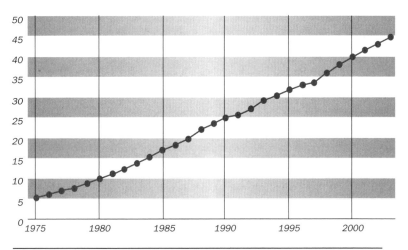

Today, baby boomers continue to drive the U.S. economy with their spending habits. Within the restaurant industry, fast food has already begun to feel the effects of this group growing older. With their children now in high school, college, and out of the nest, these consumers have returned to making their own dining-out decisions. In their prime earning years, boomers more frequently can afford full-service meals, usually opting for casual dining restaurants. With more-sophisticated palates, they often bypass plain burgers and fries in favor of ethnic ingredients and bold flavors.

Balancing these ongoing needs and changing desires—without alienating younger consumers—has become one of the biggest challenges facing fast-food marketers. Once again, America's largest and most influential generation has the potential to influence the industry well into this century.

Marketing Drivers: Household Characteristics

The growth of dual-income households is a defining characteristic of the boomer generation, and the fast-food industry has traditionally homed in on this trait. Much of this targeting, of course, aims at women, both as meal decision-makers and as consumers themselves. With careers and families to juggle, boomer women were the first to abandon the kitchen and cooking from scratch in favor of convenience and time savings. However, they have not given up the desire to provide their families with meals they can feel good about. The result is a potential guilt trip that fast-food marketers have been quick to exploit.

One of the best examples of a direct appeal to boomer women as meal-providers came from Boston Market in the late 1990s. An ad campaign with the tagline "Don't Mess with Dinner" centered on an aggressively priced meal package of roast chicken, side dishes, and dessert. In various television spots, mild-mannered women turned ferocious when the family dinner was interrupted by telemarketers and other phone calls.

Traditionally, the dinner daypart is far weaker than lunch for most fast-food restaurants. However, this has not stopped many operators, chicken and pizza in particular, from trying to leverage their suitability for the evening meal, especially as a special treat or last-minute lifesaver. In the 1990s an entire category emerged to fit this need, dubbed "convenient meal solutions" (CMS) or "home meal replacement." Ultimately, however, consumer interest waned in favor of the general concept of "takeout." Interestingly, although CMS had mixed success as a separate industry category, takeout is one of the fastest-growing areas of casual dining restaurants, such as Outback Steakhouse and Chili's Bar & Grill. Because baby boomers are the heaviest users of casual dining, it follows that they also are driving this takeout growth. Consequently, a battle for takeout dominance could be brewing between these full-service chains and fast food, with boomers as the prize.

When it comes to appealing to working women as consumers, one of the most common areas for fast-food marketers to explore is menu mix. Traditional fast-food restaurants have experienced mixed results from these efforts. Salads, for instance, have become a popular offering at most types of fast-food restaurants, from Taco Bell's taco salad to KFC's wrap sandwiches, which feature salad ingredients rolled into a tortilla. Wendy's is one of the most successful salad marketers, with its Caesar side salad proving a successful anchor to its 99-cent value menu and, new in 2002, a lineup of creative main-dish salads generating a promising response. Overall, however, sales of these "green" items represent a mere blip compared with the industry's core menu of burgers, tacos, and fried chicken pieces.

Other attempts to lure women to the counter and drive-through have proved to be some of the biggest missteps in fast-food history. In 1991, McDonald's introduced the McLean sandwich, a lower-fat and lower-calorie burger. Sales of the sandwich proved disappointing and it was soon dropped.

Despite this kind of setback, fast-food marketers are loath to give up on women, particularly boomers who, as they age, may be more sensitive to health and diet issues. In early 2002, Burger King introduced menu items that were more likely to appeal to women: a chicken version of its trademark Whopper sandwich and a meatless veggie burger. After a highly successful test run, McDonald's rolled out a fruit-and-yogurt parfait system wide.

Perhaps the most successful marketer of "healthy" fast food today is Subway. The company has surprised many with the overwhelming

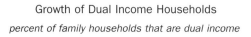

FIGURE 6.2

Growth of Dual Income Households

percent of family households that are dual income

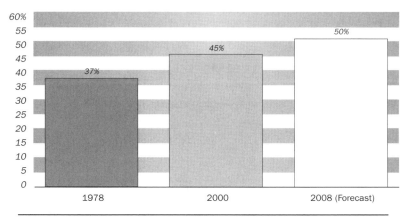

response to a recent ad campaign featuring "Jared," an obese man who achieved amazing weight loss on a diet of Subway sandwiches. Many of the chain's salads and sandwiches have always been low in fat, and nothing is fried. Using other "real-life" stories, Subway has positioned itself as a healthful fast-food choice without changing its menu or its core concept.

Arrival of Children

Children of baby boomers have presented a marketing advantage for fast-food restaurants. During the prosperity of the 1950s and 1960s, parents of boomers indulged their children. When boomers became parents, they followed that example, allowing children to influence wide-ranging purchasing decisions, especially food.

Fast-food chains have been more than eager to tap into this indulgent streak and have become perhaps the savviest child marketers outside the toy industry. Unlike what happens at most toy stores, however, parents at fast-food restaurants also make purchases for themselves—often spending twice as much on their own meals as their children's. Consequently, the stakes for the boomer child's share of stomach have been much higher than they might first appear.

The children's meal is the important element of this marketing strategy. Often priced under $2, it is sized for the small appetite and contains the restaurant's most kid-friendly menu items: chicken nuggets, french fries, and burgers. Most also come with a toy that ties into a popular television show, cartoon, or movie. These tie-ins also go beyond children's meals, targeting older children with larger toys and promotional items such as reusable cups. They usually are released at the height of the show or movie's popularity, virtually guaranteeing a lift in traffic. In perhaps the most successful kids' meal promotion ever, McDonald's distributed miniature versions of the 1990's fad Beanie Babies. The chain ran out of the items after reports of customers buying Happy Meals only for the toys and throwing away the food.

However, such a strong focus on tie-ins and toys can backfire. Taco Bell twice was burned when the expected buzz over a new movie fizzled. In addition, safety issues have arisen with the novelties included in children's meals after several choking or suffocation incidents. KFC has moved away from toys in children's meals, opting instead for educational games and a box that resembles a laptop computer. The food in the meal has gotten a makeover as well, with applesauce or fruit rollups offered instead of traditional fries or a fat-laden biscuit.

McDonald's also pioneered the concept of fast food as more than just a restaurant with its PlayPlace playgrounds. These enclosed areas allow parents to entertain and feed their children at the same time, or at least have a meal themselves while the kids work off some steam. Because of the large expense and need for space, however, these playgrounds have limited potential. In addition, as their own children have gotten older, boomers may be more likely to avoid such restaurants in a quest for peace and quiet.

As with toys, reliance on playgrounds and, to a certain degree kids themselves can cause problems from an overall marketing perspective. In the late 1990s, numerous franchisees began to complain that McDonald's had lost its focus, devoting too much attention to entertaining children and not enough to food. Indeed, research shows that a restaurant's appeal to children matters far less to most consumers than do food quality and service.

Now that the baby boom's children have gotten older, fast-food chains also are struggling with their tastes. They are too young, perhaps, for the super-sized value meals popular with adults, but too old for child-sized fries and drinks. So-called "big-kid" meals are now being attempted, although their potential may be somewhat limited given the size of this audience and finite ages to which they are targeted.

Values

Beyond household makeup, the baby boom generation has exhibited other unique characteristics on which fast-food marketers can focus. Some of these are demographic, and by far the most significant is disposable income. Others, however, have more to do with the demands and desires of mature adults who have spent their lives shaping consumer industries.

Values: income and spending

With the idea of pursuing a "career" rather than just a job, boomers have been upwardly mobile and achievement oriented. Consequently, they earn more than any generation before them, and spend more as well. As with many other discretionary purchases, disposable income drives foodservice purchases.

Because they recognize the affluence of boomers, a number of fast-food companies have thrown off the mantle of low prices that has burdened fast food for years. These companies, many of which emerged in the 1980s and 1990s, attempt to offer an "experience" rather than just a product. They focus on respecting the customer's time, offering a quick respite, not necessarily a cheap break. Moreover, they are focusing squarely on baby boomers' wallets.

Starbucks offers a prime example of this phenomenon. Before the emergence of the coffee chain, paying more than 75 cents for a cup of coffee was difficult. Now, paying less than $4 is the challenge, once the order is placed for a *vente* (large) mocha cappuccino with skim milk and whipped cream. In some of the most popular sandwich chains, such as Panera Bread and Corner Bakery, a sandwich, chips and beverage can set you back $8. Few consumers in their 20s and early 30s can afford such treats on a daily or weekly basis. For many boomers, however, price is less of an issue than the value they see in a comfortable environment and customized, made-to-order products.

Going hand-in-hand with a willingness to spend more money on fast food is the boomers' expectation of high quality. Starbucks also delivers on this front, with its premium offerings. Early on, the company pitched the idea of its baristas (coffee drink makers) as skilled professionals—a polar opposite of the stereotypical fast-food employee at the other end of the drive-through speaker. Starbucks threw away espresso drinks not served within seconds and remade them. Some consumers criticized the approach as pretentious. However, this attention to high quality at a restaurant with a check average under $5 was unique, and it clicked with baby boomers on an unprecedented level.

Starbucks is far from the only chain focusing on delivering a high-quality product, and they are not all upscale, either. KFC, for instance, launched a major advertising campaign poking fun at the image of typical fast-food burger fare as small, messy, and tasteless. The chain's own items, such as large chicken pieces and whole muscle nuggets (instead of pressed meat) are pitched as superior in quality and taste. The choice of spokesman Jason Alexander of *Seinfeld* fame also can be seen as a direct appeal to the boomer generation.

This trend toward a higher quality image is partly a result of intense competition at the low end of price-points. Few operators, especially smaller emerging concepts, can compete against the 99-cent sandwiches and value meals of the biggest chains. Many are opting instead to focus on the experience, subtly going after the self-indulgent, well-heeled consumer, an apt description of the boomer.

The rise of so-called "Quick-casual" restaurants is linked tightly to this issue of higher quality at a higher price point. The phrase "Quick-casual" was coined to describe restaurants that blend fast-food service and price points with the menu and décor elements of casual dining restaurants like Chili's and Olive Garden. An often-cited example of a Quick-casual concept is Panera Bread, mentioned above, a chain of bakeries with a café that sells sandwiches, salads, and soup as well as whole loaves of bread and other retail bakery items. The décor is decidedly upscale, with earth tones, dramatic lighting, and comfortable chairs and booths.

Since the late 1990s, numerous other companies have emerged with similar positioning, with a check average between $6 and $9. The idea behind these restaurants is to offer higher quality food and experience with the expectation that boomers are willing to pay. Names to watch in the coming years include Cosi, la Madeleine, and Noodles & Co. The latter's menu is centered on pasta, ranging from beef stroganoff to pad Thai, served in a warm, wood-enhanced dining room.

Traditional fast-food chains, smelling an opportunity to keep boomers coming back, aggressively attempted to mimic the offerings, if not the overall style, of these Quick-casual concepts. Arby's breathed new life into its concept by rolling out a new line of sandwiches, named "Market Fresh." More like the offerings at a café like Panera than its trademark roast beef on a bun, Arby's sandwiches are made on whole-grain bread and feature fillings like chicken Caesar. Subway, too, enhanced its menu to better compete with its new Quick-casual competitors. Although the chain has not done away with its signature plain, baked rolls, additional bread choices now include Asiago cheese and peppercorn flavors of artisanal-style loaves. Sister concepts, Hardee's and Carl's Jr., experienced success with what they call their "$6 burger." Although priced in the $3 range, an ad campaign that launched the sandwiches compared them with the burgers served at T.G.I.Friday's, complete with fresh toppings.

Wendy's also got into the act. The burger chain's line of salads look and taste like something off a casual dining menu. Varieties include Mandarin chicken and Chicken BLT. Perhaps even more significantly, parent company Wendy's International, which also owns the Tim Horton's donut chain, agreed to acquire the Baja Fresh chain of Mexican-style eateries and invested $9 million in Café Express, a Houston-based chain with a wide-ranging menu of roast chicken, sandwiches, salads, and pasta. Similarly, McDonald's acquired Chipotle, a Denver-based Mexican chain, selling made-to-order tacos and burritos, as well as beer and margaritas.

Such developments suggest that of all the activity occurring in fast-food today, it is the Quick-casual segment that could have the most effect on baby boomer use and the industry overall.

Values: convenience

The same drive that helped boomers devote more time to their jobs, families, and hobbies has created unprecedented demand for convenience. In fact, it is no exaggeration to say that baby boomers gave rise to the convenience industry. Before they came of age, there were no 7-Elevens, no 24-hour grocery stores and, of course, no fast-food chains. With their limited menus, quick-food assembly and drive-through windows, fast food chains present the ultimate in meal convenience.

However, such service can be considered a victim of its own success. As the standard for speed has been raised, successive improvements in wait times are harder to come by. Boomers have set the standard for overscheduled lives, from 60-hour workweeks and out-of-town business trips to training for marathons and fitting in 18 holes of golf on Saturday. Time is now considered a type of currency, and during a busy day, minutes wasted in line or waiting for an order can influence a restaurant decision. In response, fast-food restaurants are constantly searching for ways to shave even a few seconds off each transaction. One of the latest—aimed also at increasing overall convenience for affluent baby boomers—is automatic payment with car-based transponders and "debit wands" that deduct the total from the consumer's account balance. Credit card and debit card payments also are increasingly available with instant authorization.

Perhaps the most important element of convenience, however, is location. Finding suitable high-traffic locations for the baby boomer market presents a difficult challenge for the real estate divisions of major chains. As these consumers have matured and moved farther out to the suburbs, fast-food operators have followed. The resulting competition for prime real estate sites in large markets has become a major issue for most companies. Not only are many areas fully built-up, making sites scarce, but the cost for out-lots and leases in the best new areas often put them out of reach for the average franchisee. (At the end of 2002, McDonald's announced that it would begin closing some stores, perhaps an admission that at least part of the market is oversaturated.)

Co-branding is one response to this struggle for the right site. The first to try these have been so-called portfolio companies, such as Yum Brands, Inc. (formerly Tricon Global Restaurants), which owns and operates KFC, Pizza Hut, Taco Bell, Long John Silvers and A&W Restaurants. As industry consolidation results in more of these kinds of multi-concept holdings, fast-food operators are likely to increase co-branding and even tri-branding, to increase the value—and convenience to the consumer—of a single site.

Values: nostalgia

Another trend influencing the fast-food industry is nostalgia. In recent years, baby boomers have launched a wave of longing for the "good old days." Likely driven by the mid-life reckoning many are undergoing, this trend has revived interest in products from their childhoods in the 1950s and 1960s. In the fast-food industry, marketers are trying to connect with these memories (regardless of how accurate or authentic). The introduction of extra-thick milkshakes, deli-style sandwiches and other old-fashioned items are an attempt, at least in part, to court the more mature customer.

Sonic Drive-In is a good example. The chain has gained a dominant position in the ultra-competitive hamburger category in part by maintaining such old-fashioned elements as carhop service, customized soft drinks like cherry limeade and "cream pie" milkshakes. A&W, a similar concept with a longer history and the bonus of a well-known brand (of root beer), also revels in its vintage image.

Other regional burger chains are trying to tap into this interest. Backyard Burgers, based in Mississippi, positions its burgers and chicken sandwiches as tasting like they were cooked on a backyard grill—à la the 1960s. The chain claims its customers value quality over price, which helps it maintain one of the highest check averages in the industry. In-N-Out Burgers has developed a cult-like following in California and Nevada for its bare-bones menu, which features nothing more than burgers (made from fresh beef), fresh hand-cut fries, and milk shakes.

Perhaps the most successful fast-food restaurant capitalizing on the wave of nostalgia is Krispy Kreme Donuts. A darling of Wall Street since its initial public offering in 2000, Krispy Kreme has leveraged its decades-old roots as a Southern institution. Although the core product is nothing more than fried dough and sugar, transplanted consumers are reported to weep at their first taste in years when a unit opens in a new market. The hype surrounding the chain's aggressive expansion is more likely driven by a slick public relations machine than by true love of the donuts. Nevertheless, the image in the public's mind—particularly boomer minds—is that of an American classic.

That these menu items also appeal to younger consumers should not obscure the fact that baby boomers are a key target of this type of food and service. In fact, cross-generational marketing may prove to be a successful strategy, as boomers reject the notion of aging like their parents.

Food Tastes

While disposable income and demands for quality and convenience all influence restaurant decisions, the ultimate reason consumers dine out is to eat. As they have with virtually all other attributes of the fast-food industry, boomers have had a profound impact on the food being served. As their tastes have changed and influenced younger genera-tions, fast food has tried to keep pace. The result was a wave of menu innovation that brought new flavors and ingredients to the table, par-ticularly in the past decade. Burgers and fries are still the most popu-lar fast-food items by far, but others edging up the list are beginning to make it a contest. Entire concepts developed around a unique offer-ing, such as fish tacos or juice smoothies, have become viable busi-nesses. In general, these changes reflect the increasingly sophisticated palate of the baby boomer, and many more developments can be expected in this most dynamic area of foodservice.

Food tastes: ethnic foods

Not many years ago, pushing the envelope of exotic cuisine meant try-ing Szechuan Chinese food instead of Cantonese. Even today, the most popular ethnic cuisines in the U.S.—by a wide margin—are Mexican, Italian, and Chinese. Thanks in large part to the baby boom genera-tion, some of the most popular appetizers in restaurants are quesadil-las, pot stickers, and calamari. The "mainstreaming" of these and other items, like croissants and even sushi, reflects the boomer's own travel experiences and interest in other cultures. After all, this generation made *The Food Lover's Guide to Paris* a bestseller.

Typically, food trends first appear among cutting-edge chefs, then later are picked up by casual dining restaurants and finally appear in fast food. True to form, interest in and demand for ethnic foods has finally trickled down to the drive-through window. The Quick-casual restaurants described previously in this chapter are on the front lines of this march toward ethnic flavors. Many, particularly those with a Mexican bent, position themselves as more "authentic" alternatives to traditional fast food. Baja Fresh, for example, sells fish and shrimp tacos and offers customers a self-service condiment bar with freshly made salsas and chopped cilantro. Pei Wei, the quick-service concept opened by casual dining operator P. F. Chang's, features menu items such as Asian Coconut Curry and salted soybeans in the pod. Others simply borrow from various ethnic cuisines without committing to a single country. Tandoori chicken wraps are served next to Cuban pork sandwiches.

Today, even McDonald's is experimenting with ethnic flavor profiles, such as milkshakes flavored with "dulce de leche," a Hispanic caramel that has become de rigeur for sweet tooth fanatics. The American population, including baby boomers, is becoming more ethnically diverse, and with that diversity comes a growing demand for authentic foods. It also is true that Generations X and Y show a greater willingness to try ethnic foods than any other age group. However, the wide popularity of ethnic foods indicates that interest clearly goes beyond racial and generational lines, expanding into the mainstream after being fueled by the boomer generation. Moreover, boomers will continue to support the most innovative ethnic food trends among both independent chefs and traditional fast-food restaurants.

Food tastes: bold flavors

Just as baby boomers were the first American generation to embrace ethnic cuisines, they also were the first to cultivate a sophisticated palate. In this respect, the U.S. lags several generations behind many European and Asian countries, but thanks to the boomers, it is making up for lost time. The organic movement of the 1970s helped focus attention on food as more than just sustenance—as something to be respected as well. In the 1980s, a crop of young American chefs lifted the reputation of the country's own cuisine instead of just mimicking the French or Italian.

By the 1990s, cable television had launched the Food Network channel, targeting baby boomers 24-hours a day with personalities like

Emeril Lagasse whipping up jambalaya.

What does all this have to do with the fast-food industry? As noted in the rise of ethnic cuisines, food trends will eventually make their way down to the major chains. Already, particularly in the Quick-casual arena, there is a clear focus on ingredients with distinctive character and bold flavors, like Asiago cheese, roasted garlic, cilantro, and chipotle peppers. Even traditional chains are trying to put more oomph into their menus. Popeye's Chicken & Biscuits, for instance, includes Creole Chicken Etouffee, part of a recently launched Louisiana Legends section of the menu.

Outlook for the Future

As the bulk of the boomer generation hits middle age and their retirement years, the consumer market stands ready to react. Here are some possibilities:

- In the fast-food arena, as well as foodservice in general, these consumers may see bolder flavors designed to tickle aging taste buds.

- Portion-size options may multiply, as older Americans seek to watch their health more closely and as appetites shift with age. Yet, some chains will continue to feature large portions, i.e. Cheesecake Factory.

- Special menu items or menu combinations could be unveiled for diabetics or those watching sodium intake.

- Even menu boards could get bigger, offering bifocal wearers an easier time when ordering.

Traditionally, Americans over age 55 have been and continue to be the lightest users of fast food. This is not surprising, given their reduced incomes and their diminished need for time savings. However, as the boomer generation ages, many predict that the behavior of the group over age 55 will change. After decades of saving and investing, some boomers are better prepared economically for retirement than previous generations. Among some, the idea of retirement will not be to slow down or cut back, but rather to finally indulge in all the activities that have been sacrificed for careers and for family rearing.

These active retirees cannot be expected to retreat back into the kitchen. Neither will they want to drop $50 on dinner out every night. Rather, it is highly likely these consumers will continue to rely on fast food, particularly Quick-casual concepts, as an affordable indulgence that provides convenience and time savings. So far, it does not appear that fast-food marketers are targeting the near-retiree. This is not surprising, given the fact that the peak of the baby boom generation will not reach age 50 until 2007. A decade from now, however, it will likely be a different story.

7

Baby Boomers and Technology: Selling the "Me" Generation New Toys

Michelle Edelman
Chief Planning Officer, LB Works, Chicago

The perpetually youthful mindset of the baby boomer generation means that even though they weren't born of "the internet generation," they are the largest, most affluent, most gadget-grabbing generation in American history. Boomers have fully embraced technology. They are among the most optimistic about the pure promise of technology, what it will do for them and how it can change the world for the better.

Thus, they are actively seeking ways to integrate technology into their lives. As such, they drive a significant share of volume and dollar value into the technology category all by themselves. More-

Baby boomers are the largest, most affluent, most gadget-grabbing generation in American history.

over, baby boomers control not only their own wallets, but have significant say over the budgets of others such as their parents, children, and friends. Amazingly, in this light, they represent the single biggest purchase-and-influence segment for technology-driven products.

However, an analysis of technology industry marketing and advertising would indicate quite the opposite. Marketers, who are trying to grab the mindshare and future spending potential of a younger crowd, largely overlook baby boomers. The surface reasoning is clear: Echo boomers represent nearly as big a population as the baby boomers. They are growing up with technology as

Michelle Edelman is senior vice president and chief planning officer for LB Works, 35 W. Wacker Drive, Chicago, IL 60601; 312-220-6969; michelle.edelman@lbworks.com, www.lbworks.com.

a passive influence on everything around them, and will be in a great position to become "customers for life" if influenced early. Baby boomers, on the other hand, seem to have been poster children of the rapid metamorphosis of technology. They have laser-disc units collecting dust in their closets. They believed marketing's claims, but found that the products and services generally did not live up to them. Aren't they more difficult to sell and convince than the blank-page youth?

Research here will show you that as a technology marketer, you should be thinking about capturing more of the money and imagination of the boomers. The underlying optimism of the boomers makes them perpetually prone to spending on this category, where the premise is about improving the future. Many of today's technology marketers are boomers themselves and have a unique capacity to easily stretch their brand preferences across generations. Currently, most technology marketing does not bother speaking to boomers in the language and with the information necessary to capture their interest. We will examine boomers and technology in this chapter, and show you some tangible ways to reach them.

Technology's Biggest Influencers

Boomers are the most likely age segment to have a personal computer in their homes already. In our research, we asked groups from each age segment how they funded their current home computers. We found out:

- 82 percent of the Echo Boomers were using computers that either still belong to or used to belong to their boomer parents.

- 24 percent of Gen Xers polled stated they purchased the same brand of computer as their parents.

- 37 percent of Matures said their boomer children had given them their old computers; another 21 percent said their boomer children had purchased their computers for them as a gift.

The boomers were the only audience who for the most part (92 percent) claimed to have purchased their own household computers and very few (9 percent) will admit that people outside their generation had significantly influenced their choice of brand.

Further, the boomers we talked to prided themselves on doing the most in-depth research prior to buying a computer. On average, they spent 2.5 hours more than any other segment per purchase. Moreover, we also found that boomers were likely to pay more for the average computer purchase—on average $50 more—and were likely to replace their computers more quickly (3.2 years cycle time versus 4+ years for other segments).

This purchase-price-to-hours-of-research ratio did not make sense to us at first. One would think that an individual doing more research on a purchase would be doing so to drive down total cost of purchase. However, the additional research hours ended up correlating to the sophistication of the system purchased. Overall, boomers felt their research was getting them the best price, but on a system that was more fully loaded with software and with the latest processors and higher quality peripherals than they believed they would purchase when they started their research. For example, boomers were three times more likely to purchase a color printer over black and white, and to make that decision during the investigative process rather than beforehand.

The only area in which boomers lagged any other segment in purchasing was in the area of audio-video oriented peripherals. Boomer computers were fully 35 percent *less likely* to be equipped with joysticks, video upload devices, external microphones, separate speakers, and larger monitors, according to Yankelovich Monitor. The bottom line is that boomers are "all work" on their computers. This is not to say that the home computer is used strictly for career-related activity, but that boomers are the group most likely to be using their computers as productivity tools. This group is far more likely to routinely use their computers for personal finance and correspondence than any other functions.

Boomers routinely use their computers for personal finance and correspondence, far more than for any other functions.

All Work and No Play?

Looking at the boomer profile, one would think they bought the PC equivalent of a BMW, only to drive it in the slow lane. This is not so. It is merely that the makeup of the computers is more businesslike. They do not contain purchased software and hardware that is used for recreational activity.

Boomers are also driving a huge amount of e-commerce in retail. The generation that made paper catalogues a daily item in the mailbox, is transitioning that behavior to the web. Media Metrix reports:

- The "average" internet shopper is age 42 and male.

- Boomers represent the fastest growing internet demographic.

- They tend to surf the internet more frequently, remain online longer, and check out a more diverse array of internet pages than their college-age counterparts.

The younger boomer segment is also more likely to conduct online banking than any other segment. They are more likely to indulge in grocery delivery, online travel booking, and online gift purchasing than any other segment. The overloaded lifestyle of the younger boomers in their 40s has spawned a convenience industry on the internet that piques the interest of this generation.

Computers Are Good

Therefore, this box in the office is now more like a conduit that makes life easier. This contributes to boomers' highly optimistic view of technology. As we will explore later in depth, the older boomer segment is a bit more wary of technology as "Big Brother," but despite its fears the whole generation tends toward a more idealistic view of how technology can improve people's lives.

When we asked our panel about what computers could do for them:

- 41 percent more boomers than any other generation talked unaided about computers saving lives in the form of hospital machines.

- 82 percent talked about the change in their lives because of embedded processors in cars, ovens, toys, and other common items. Younger people were less likely to have perceived this shift; older people were less likely to trust or own the updated versions of the originals.

- 23 percent more boomers than any other generation confess to be taken in by "The Making Of" television documentaries on robotics, computers, and technology.

There is clearly a fascination with technology in general among this generation, which is explained in more detail in our in-depth interviews later in the chapter.

But Computers Are also Bad

As an interesting contrast, though we were not initially seeking this information, boomers volunteered their frustrations with computers and technology as well:

- 47 percent volunteered feelings of frustrations with their computers at least weekly.

- 23 percent volunteered feelings of frustration with other chip-enabled consumer electronics (like programmable microwaves, for example) at least weekly.

- More than half (54 percent) of frustrated respondents said that being "fed up" with the computer or device has made them hesitate about making a purchase either at the time of the frustration or when they consider to expanding or upgrading the system or product.

In fact, this study had a higher incidence of people writing volumes on this subject in the "Anything Else We Forgot to Ask?" box than any study in recent memory! Therefore, we polled our panel further on their negative feelings.

In general, boomers have a hard time separating software issues from hardware issues. Software incompatibility, a missing font, a mouse that isn't recognized by the system, all are seen as "problems with my computer." The box takes the blame for most ills.

Further, when boomers try to rectify these problems, they find the manuals too complicated, the support websites hard to navigate, and the telephone personnel either impossible to reach or speaking in terms they don't understand. This leaves a highly intelligent, educated, moneyed person feeling intellectually neutered.

In addition, because of their lack of advanced knowledge about "what's in there," boomers are susceptible to scares about security of their information and systems. Everything from credit card fraud to viruses are top of mind for this group. The lack of understandable information about these instances makes them feel more vulnerable than they like.

These fears and frustrations don't quell the generation's quest for more, newer, and better, but it does make them more cautious about trying new things or systems.

Fans of the Industry

Boomers are also a group who have followed the rise of the technology industry and who count as some of their personal folk heroes, members of their own generation who were or are heads of computer companies.

- Boomers were 3.2 times more likely to admire Steve Jobs, Bill Gates, Larry Ellison, or Lou Gerstner, among other business icons, than they were movie stars or politicians.

- Generation Xers, and younger were more likely to admire pop stars while Matures admire statesmen.

Boomers could more consistently and correctly name Bill Gates, Steve Jobs, Larry Ellison, and other business icons from a picture sort than they could their own senators!

Bill Gates	*Larry Ellison*	*Dick Durbin*
Chairman, Microsoft	*CEO, Oracle*	*Democratic Senator for*
		Illinois at time of study

The boomers we talked to made it clear that their personal fortunes were made (and in some cases, broken!) in a significant way by these business icons. To them, no other group of people in recent memory have had more influence over the growth of their personal wealth than technology industry leaders. They are 89 percent more likely than their younger and older counterparts to be consistently reading the Technology section of their favorite newspapers and keeping up with emerging points of view and technologies, though their brand recognition is more with the larger and more established players.

As well, at the upper-income bracket of the boomer category, we found a close correlation with willingness to purchase a computer or software from companies whose stock is listed in one's personal portfolio.

The Emotional Connection

Clearly, in our quantitative and secondary research we found some interesting attraction to technology and technology concepts. We then wanted to relate this to boomers more qualitatively as they progress through the decades.

We start this section with some key observations and themes that repeated themselves through the qualitative research, and are fundamental ideas that many researchers and planners have touched on over the years when studying the boomers.

Boomers feel they will redefine the process of aging, and that technology is their partner in this pursuit.

Their perpetually youthful attitude is leading boomers to explore ways to stay young, in every sense of the word. They realize that technology is their ally in doing so. From designer drugs to instant travel bargains over the internet, they will continue to embrace and exploit technology to keep them up with the times.

Boomers feel they created the idea of modern freedom, but that freedom has brought with it exploitation, extremism, and ironically enough, apathy.

Without exception, the boomers we talked to reminded us that they remember a time when commerce, politics, human rights, and many other basic standard-of-living issues were more constrained than they are now, and in some cases, unacceptably so. They proudly talk about their role in defending and making the world a better and more equal place. They then quickly move to discussing how the following generations (or even those in their generation who were not catalysts for change) have not understood the great value in these achievements. Most felt that their contributions had led to systematic abuse, and a disregard of what life might be like without them.

Boomers are prone to messages about how hard things used to be and how much better technology has made it.

Boomers talk about technology in the same light. They feel that life today holds many conveniences that their children take for granted and exploit. They decry the era of video games and wish youth valued more pursuits for the social good. They feel they are more conscious, appreciative, and wary of the true value of technology, having lived in the world both with and without it. They are therefore prone to messages about how hard things used to be and how much better technology has made it.

Boomers feel they created the world in which advancements in technology could occur, yet they feel these advancements are geared "to younger people" and that they are messaged out of the loop.

For the most part, boomers feel "out of it." They feel their children were born into the "tech" generation, and that most products and services are created with them in mind. This confuses them, considering they also feel they created the commercial opportunity and core ideas on which today's technology is based. They want to be included in the newest wave of what's happening with these innovations, but it is hard for them to relate to the situations and people presented to them in typical messages about these products and services.

Boomers feel they are perceived as inflexible and hard to teach.

The truth is that the older the boomer, the more they admit difficulty in learning and embracing new technologies and devices. There does come a point when maximizing what one does well and not taking on new technologies year after year is favored behavior. As well, the boomers have more sharply defined gender roles than do younger generations; the men are more likely to use their computers for finance, for example, whereas women are big users in correspondence and home-work aides.

However, the boomers' intense optimism about technology and improvement of life leads them to the well repeatedly. They feel they apply themselves to learning more conscientiously than their younger and older counterparts. They were taught to learn from teachers who broadcast information to them in traditional classrooms, yet find no such learning implements for technologies. They seek human contact in order to learn new skills, and feel that this frustrates their younger counterparts who are most often in the position of teaching them. Boomers feel that most computing companies have missed the boat on how they best learn and that these companies simply don't understand that remote learning (CRT or handbook) or learn-as-you-go methods aren't effective for them.

Boomers feel they simply have higher standards for communication.

The boomers we talked to say they are turned off by recent years' trends toward vulgarity and "overproduced" advertising in technology marketing, and are intimidated by the mounting alter-dictionary of acronyms they encounter. They can appreciate the beauty of models rotating dreamily and in vivid color in a high-tech washing machine, but they feel disconnected to the idea and ultimately don't understand how this is supposed to make them feel. They have a very functional approach to advertising and communication when it comes to new technologies. They like to be told the main benefits in a straightfor-ward way and feel as peers with the brand or company that's selling to them. They are comfortable with either clean simplicity (like Apple Computer's television commercials) or detailed explanatory messaging (like Dell Computer's print advertising). These are universal feelings from boomers across the age breaks.

Now let's look at the results of the qualitative research that focused on representatives in three different phases of life: Family Time, Empty Nest, and Retired or Semi-Retired. We found in our quantitative work that these life stage breaks were the simplest way to differentiate atti-tude and use of technology. We then explored the differences and the reasons for them by working with individuals who are currently in each of the different phases.

Meet Jim, The Family Guy

My name's Jim. I'm 37 years old and live in New Jersey. I work at a bank in Manhattan and commute there every day.

I have two girls, ages 9 and 5. My wife quit her job to stay home with them when our youngest was born and she's pretty much busy with their activities all day.

We have a home computer, and I have a different computer at work. I have a Palm Pilot, we have three cell phones in the house, and I think everything we own has a computer chip inside it!

This is how Jim introduced himself at our focus groups, after which we asked Jim if we could follow up with him in depth. Jim typifies the younger boomer who is in the Family Time stage of life. His life is all about going to work, coming home, spending time with the kids, squeezing in friends, and then doing it all over again. His weekday routine is very predictable. He works in a large office complex, and uses his home life as a cocoon away from the outside world.

Jim talked about his computers, phones, and PalmPilot as the top-of-mind pieces of technology he uses, but the more he talked, the more he realized that everything in his life is dependent on technology.

- If the electricity in Jim's house shut down, he thinks nothing in the house would work at all including all clocks.

- His cars are completely computerized and have the latest gadgets, without which the cars he currently loves would seem a bit primitive and uninteresting to him.

- He uses the internet for more hours a day than the television, a fact he did not initially believe was true until he kept a journal of his time on both during our study.

- He does not bank online, but uses software programs to keep financial records for his family.

- Jim counted the number of technology upgrades or new purchases across a three-month period and came up with 27, from new versions of software to extra batteries to gifts for others.

Yet, Jim remembers when this was clearly not the case. He doesn't necessarily remember how things got so integrated and abundant, but he does remember what it was like to live without these things.

Technology powers our lives. I'm sure it overcomplicates them, too. I remember when I first saw a fax machine. I was working at a restaurant one summer and the boss brought it in. He was so proud of it. It was the fastest way to send something written at the time. We thought it would never catch on because it never rang and we really couldn't send anything. Nobody else had one! Now everyone has at least two e-mail addresses. The pace of things is more out of control.

Jim's home computer sits on a desk in his office. Jim and his wife consider it a piece of office equipment and his daughters consider it a gaming and communications device. They don't claim to have a lot of contention over the use of the computer, but this is mostly because they feel naturally compelled to use the computer at different times. Jim's wife generally uses the computer while her kids are at school. Jim uses it on the weekends when the kids are with friends or outside. The kids have an agreed-to schedule during the week so they can share the computer and limit their time.

The kids talk about "going on the computer," while the adults take more of a task orientation (go to ftd.com, balance the checkbook, write a note to mom). This parallels the way they refer to their telephone; the kids say they "want to get on the phone," while the parents talk about calling mom or checking work voice mail.

Jim's relationship with his computer is most interesting when viewed through the following lenses:

• **Keeping up with the kids.**

Jim has an interest and fascination in watching his kids work with the computer. They appear much more comfortable with everything about it than he does; his 5-year-old can install her own games when she gets them from the store now. However, he can see that this comfort is also making his kids more sedentary.

If I let my kids stay online and on the computer for all their free time, they would! It's more mesmerizing than the TV for them. They really aren't as interested in the stuff I used to be interested in, like running around, going to the playground, or shopping or something. They would rather interact with the computer than live people sometimes.

As well, Jim worries about what the kids are doing, learning, and who they are with online.

It's an unknown. I used to be nervous about the kids' peer groups and how I would handle it if I really didn't like their friends. Now I am faced with not ever really knowing who those people are that they're communicating with, never setting eyes on them. They may not be in our community or in their age group. It's a hard thing to control and manage as a parent.

Jim is therefore interested in turning his kids' computer affinity into a hobby that takes them offline, and in turning more of their computer time into homework time. What's interesting is that while he appreciates and admires his daughter's growing adeptness with the computer as a tool, he is not comfortable with the computer as a communications device. He is conscious of the "digital generation gap" not in terms of what he has bought, but how it is deployed.

Boomers may be conscious of the "digital generation gap" in terms of how computers are used.

• **Spending on toys.**

Jim is addicted to the Best Buy circular. He delights in reviewing what is new, and what is on sale. He develops boredom with his current system and envy of others rather quickly.

We have some discretionary income, and I don't mind spending it on gadgets. For example, we recently bought a digital camera. I guess we didn't really need it, but it just seemed like such a convenience not to have to deal with film and developing on vacation. Now I am thinking we need to replace our cell phones. It's funny, it seems like I get a hankering for something once a month. For me, the fun is in the hunt.

Jim also tends to check out deals on things he has already bought.

I look to see what they're selling my PC for now. I don't know why, it's almost like I'm waiting to be ripped off after the fact. Most of the time, whenever I get something, it drops 10 percent in price within 6 months, or the company starts giving a cash rebate. I always kick myself, but my wife says I have gotten use and enjoyment out of it all this time, why should I be upset? I know that this is true, yet I am still compelled to check out the prices.

This drives Jim to typically specify the higher-end equipment that makes him think he is:

- Getting more system for the money,
- Getting something that nobody else has, or
- Getting something he thinks is ahead enough in the market that it will hold its value for some time.

When Jim reflected on this behavior and his motivations, he was frustrated with himself and did not understand quite why this highly speculative cycle was occurring, but because he has so much fun in the window-shopping phase, he is unlikely to modify his behavior.

- **Indulging in insider information.**

Jim knows five people with careers in information technology. These people are around his age, and he tends to consult them for advice on products to buy and for news on the industry.

I don't own a lot of technology stocks, but the ones I bought over the years, I got tips on from my friends in the industry. I'm not sure if they've performed better or worse than any random thing in my mutual funds, but I feel more confident buying them because of these guys I know.

Jim's friends give him intimate knowledge about the way that their companies operate, which seems to give him more confidence about researching and purchasing products and services.

One of my buddies told me that tech companies treat their customers better if they buy extended service. So I always make sure I sign up for whatever loyalty program or elite service they have. And, I think

I do spend less time on hold and people respond to me more quickly.

In everyday situations, Jim's friends tend to compare notes about their electronic equipment. Examples of this Jim noted in his journal:

- During a golf game, his friends were comparing cellular phone models and service prices.

- After a business lunch, work acquaintances beamed each other their business cards and personal contact information using their handheld devices.

- While waiting for a train, Jim struck up a conversation with a stranger about his brand of laptop computer.

This casual exchange of information gives Jim a passive knowledge of what is new, how to formulate his preferences, and generally confirms his satisfaction about the purchase decisions about the products he did buy.

- **Infusing the internet into every day.**

It would be inaccurate to call Jim a surfing addict. However, in addition to using the internet in his workplace for corporate activity, Jim does use the internet for everyday things he used to obtain in other ways only a few years ago. Examples of items sought on a daily basis, and usually several times per day:

- Weather forecast
- Maps and directions
- School and other activity schedules
- Addresses and phone numbers
- Stock and news updates

Jim feels that this activity has naturally curtailed the actions he used to take to obtain this same information, including:

- Decreased use of telephone operator-assisted services and corresponding calls to people and places of business for hours of operation and driving directions.

- Decreased use of the yellow- and white-page telephone directo-
ries in his home to the point where Jim feels he could actually
live without these resources completely.

The one thing Jim noted had not changed was his reliance on
television and newspaper media. He uses the internet to update his
knowledge between his daily newspaper and TV news appoint-
ments.

In addition to this daily dose, here are some places Jim visits at
least once per week:

- Movie listings and local event calendars

- His company's home page

- A few favorite airlines to check out vacation specials (not that
he's going anywhere!)

- Some special interest websites such as *Consumer Reports,
National Geographic,* and *Kiplinger's*

- Then there are websites that Jim visits less often. We estimated
that Jim visits over 100 websites per month, but only 10 percent
with any regularity. Other common occasions where Jim turns to
the web:
    - *Purchase clothing, books, music, and "bargains" of all types*
    - *Research a news event*
    - *Research something he has a general question about
    (a health issue, for example)*
    - *Check out a website a friend or colleague told him about*

Though Jim does not regularly visit any one online store, he does
make a purchase online at least four times a month. He feels the ability to purchase on the internet has curtailed his use of shopping malls
(which he sees as positive) and makes buying more a constant in his
life, instead of "reserved for weekends," as it was prior to having internet access at home.

The sites of his favorite retailers are online places where Jim spends
significant time (more than 5 minutes). At other sites, Jim may take a
cursory look but click away after 5 seconds or so. Jim estimates that
another 50 to 75 websites may fall into this category, primarily because

these websites came up as a result of a search-engine query but were not really what he was anticipating once he arrived.

He does have a favorite search engine and has made this his home page. He does not have many bookmarks; rather, he remembers the URLs of his favorite sites and types them in each time. When we asked why he did things this way, he said he just forgets about the bookmark feature. In fact, Jim really does not use the majority of the features of his browser. He only routinely uses the "back," "forward," and "stop" buttons and really has not explored the other features, though he has used the same browser brand for over four years.

Conclusions about Jim

Jim has clearly integrated technology into his daily life and gains mostly positive experiences and emotions from interacting with technology. Though he is conscious that there are other ways of accomplishing the same tasks, he enjoys the experience technologies bring to him, causing him to associate a higher monetary value with these activities. He feels a generation gap with his children over the use of technology and is aware that while enjoyment is technology's main role in his life, it technology seems inseparable from tasks for his children and much more autonomic.

Meet Linda, the Empty Nester

> *I'm really amazed at the way technology has made its way into my life. I was the kind of person who dreaded when the power would go out and I would have to reprogram the time on the VCR! But now I feel like I've found a good balance with a lot of automated things.*

Linda is 49. Her youngest daughter recently graduated from high school. Though both she and her husband still work full time, she finds herself with a lot more time on her hands than she ever had. She was a perfect subject to follow in the mid-age range of boomers, and her actions and attitudes were much like her peers in this stage of her life. She tends to have a regimented schedule during the workday, but on weekends her time is very much her own. She is suddenly faced with how she personally wants to spend that time, providing her with an opportunity to discover her passions, but also with a bit of an empty feeling.

One of the results of this transition is that her computer is playing a different role in her life than it used to.

I used to see my computer as something I would use for work, or to help the kids with homework, or type up a quick list. Now I am really starting to explore the internet. There's a lot out there about travel, gardening, baking . . . lots of the things I'm starting to take up again.

So to Linda, her computer has become a conduit to a whole new world she's trying to explore. Linda works at a hospital where she has another computer. In addition, in Linda's household there are:

* Two cell phones

* A pager (for her husband's work)

* Many chip-driven appliances, like microwave ovens and stereo equipment

Interestingly, Linda felt just as strongly as Jim that technology touches every aspect of her life. However, she has far less variety in the technology equipment in her house and in her life, and that equipment is far less integrated into her life. She prefers her conventional oven to her microwave. She doesn't keep her wireless phone on except when she needs to place a call. While they are all around her, the gadgets are used by choice, not by nature.

Linda's most interesting lenses are:

* **Using the internet as a wider social and personal community.**

Though she has a computer at work and one at home, Linda uses the internet strictly at home. However, she is using the internet as a research and purchasing tool to open up new horizons for her in her evolving lifestyle. For example, Linda is starting to pay more attention to herself physically. The internet provides her with some outlets for setting new daily regimens.

I have never been one for exercising or paying attention to what I ate. However, I am starting to read more about osteoporosis since my mother started ailing from it. There is a whole world of prevention that I can provide for myself at this age, for a whole bunch of older women's diseases. So I've started to do things differently one by one. I found a website where I could program a diet for myself and order vitamins. It was very easy to do, easy to read because the type was large and the diet was personalized for me using my health background. It was so much easier and more valuable than a doctor's visit.

In addition, Linda has become dependent on her e-mail to hear from her kids and distant family.

It's easier to get them to write me an e-mail than to call me on the phone. They are busy and studying all the time, I know that, and they can write me a note at 1 in the morning when they would never want to call here. Also, I am getting closer with my sister, who's older than me and living in Arizona, through our e-mail exchanges. We exchange pictures and just feel closer. It's really so nice to open up my e-mail and have a few messages waiting.

Because of this shift in computer use from software packages to communications device, Linda has started to really understand online services.

I didn't use to think about it too much before. But it does seem like having the right internet service is really important. I used to have a small local service. It didn't cost a lot, but sometimes it was very difficult to get online and the connection was slow or would disconnect a lot. So I went to the place I bought my computer and asked them what to do. They told me to change services and recommended which one I might like. Later when I got home, I looked at websites for the different services. America Online seemed like it was the easiest to use and also the most fun. Some of the others seemed too technical for me. So I changed services and I'm much happier. I even get a lot of extra information I can use from America Online about travel and some other things I'm interested in.

Therefore, Linda estimates her internet usage has risen about

15 percent since the change in ISP. Her bill each month has doubled, but she still claims she's getting good service for a reasonable
price.

*I don't think you could pay any less than I'm paying and still get
good service.*

- **Using the internet to expand her horizons away from the
computer.**

Since it's just Linda and her husband now, the urge to be more
spontaneous with their leisure time has blossomed into new purchasing habits.

Empty Nesters' purchasing habits change with their new freedom.

*It gets to be Thursday, and we start to think, could we get
tickets to something? Or even get away someplace? Get a hotel
room and drive down to see one of the kids, or a bed and
breakfast an hour away we've never been to? I guess we could
plan in advance, but somehow, it gets to be Thursday and
we're in a mad rush to do something new and different.*

In addition, Linda has more of an urge to splurge.

*We work hard and now's our time to enjoy! So I've been doing lit-
tle things, like getting box seats instead of the less expensive ones. It's
just so much nicer. I feel like we're dating again, but this time, with
money.*

The longing for premium services and experiences on a whim
drives Linda to seek last minute bargains. She talks about being
conditioned not to pay more than absolutely necessary for things—
to price shop and wait for sales. This brings up another powerful
use of the internet.

*I can really play hardball with hotels now that I know the lowest
they'll go on a room rate! I use six or seven travel websites and it's
a game to pit their prices against each other for what we want. So
this way, we pay the average price of a regular room . . . but get a
really great room. Or we get a regular room for far less than the
standard price. This allows us to order a really nice bottle of wine*

with dinner, or stay an extra night. The system I use gives us so much more freedom to get more out of what we do.

Linda's "system" is a series of carefully set up bookmarks that she visits all the time. Linda admits a coworker first showed her how to bookmark and explained the benefit; before that she was using a written list of URLs that she would type in. From looking at Linda's bookmarks, her lifestyle is simple to analyze. She sees the internet primarily through the window of these websites. She will check out others if she hears about them from a trusted source, like a friend who shares the same interests or a respected TV news reporter. However, she holds new websites to a very tough standard.

If they aren't really easy to read, easy to figure out how to use, or have something that's new or different than one of my favorites . . . then what's the point? Maybe I could save a couple extra dollars—I doubt it, but maybe—but it would cost me so much more in time. I can judge a new website in about 5 minutes.

- **Comfort is an extremely high barrier to purchase.**

It is fair to say that Linda dreads purchasing electronic equipment. Once she has it and is comfortable with it, she considers it to be like a friend or a trusted tool, but the buying process is painful.

I really don't like shopping for new computers. I know we have to every few years because everything changes so quickly and we need to be able to take advantage of all the speed and convenience the new models give us. But I really feel like computer companies and salespeople talk over my head on purpose. I never really know if I'm getting my questions answered. Do I need a color inkjet printer or should I spend a little more for a laser printer? What's the difference, really? They can tell you what the technical differences are, but nobody will tell me what the real tradeoffs are for the way I use my computer. And that's just a simple example. I have yet to hear a good explanation of what RAM and ROM are. It bugs me. What am I paying all this money for, exactly?

Linda is considering a Macintosh for her next purchase. She knows this will mean a learning curve for the software, but the principle of simplicity and a computer she can understand has a magnetic appeal. In the absence of a brand allegiance at the moment, Linda shops for new systems based strictly on speed, price, and accessories included.

I know most computers are at least going to function okay. And I know that a lot of what I do requires a faster computer . . . faster connection speed. So I usually try to get as fast as I can for the money. And then I look at what else they are throwing into the package . . . what's in there for free that's going to prevent me from spending more money on things I can't understand?

For example, Linda talked for awhile about the computer mouse. She could not understand why anyone would want to purchase a different mouse than what was included with the computer. She compared this to purchasing a different fender for a new car just for something slightly different.

• **Underlying distrust of computers.**

While Linda can explain and actually derive great benefit from her computer, at the same time she is a little wary of it. This trepidation is most pronounced at work.

I use my work computer to write up patient reports, mostly. It's like a little typewriter and file cabinet all in one. But I always make sure to copy all that stuff on diskettes. I have a drawer full of them. What if something happened to my computer? How would I get my records back?

She continued by talking about how fascinated and scared she is of all the computers that run the hospital systems.

It really is unbelievable how much of a hospital is now run by computers. When I started 25 years ago, everything was paper records, and doctors relied on their judgment, training, and skill to treat people. Now drugs are dispensed by computer. All the vital signs are monitored on computers. Every record we have is on a computer.

Well, I believe computers can mess up. People can too. The difference is that people care and take accountability. What happens if the computer misreads a blood test and a patient is treated incorrectly because of it? It's like we have invented a world where we can't do anything anymore without computers . . . and I think human judgment is better than computer knowledge.

Conclusions about Linda

Technology plays a very active and vital role in Linda's life. In fact, it is a lifeline socially. But Linda perceives herself as very separate from it and while somewhat reliant on it, is afraid of this reliance. She doesn't derive enjoyment out of technology, rather she is using it as a conduit to enjoy other things. The buying experience is intimidating to her.

She doesn't derive enjoyment from technology, rather she uses it as a conduit to enjoy other things.

Meet Ray, Nearly Retired

I have used a computer at work for a couple of years now, but really only got one for home last year. Before, we had my son's old computer and it just sat in my office, never turned it on. Never really understood why I should. But now I'm really enjoying this new one.

This year, at age 59, Ray decided to take his company's offer and formally retire. Now he works part time as a consultant for this same company through a third party contract business that provides the company with part time workers. He works fewer hours, has less responsibility and no more worries about moving up the corporate ladder. He is also taking a long look ahead.

For the first time, it's sinking in that in a few years we will be living on a fixed income. It's kind of a shock, because since the kids all got married and moved away, we've been a little more free with our spending than we used to be. Time to go on a money diet!

At the same time, Ray feels the urge to get out and enjoy his extra time. He has identified some hobbies he really enjoys and is starting to spend more concentrated periods of time on these hobbies. He joined a chess club—a passion of his from his youth, and he has started swimming in the lap pool at his community center every other day. He and his wife are thinking about selling their single-family home and moving into a condominium complex in their town. He plans to work part time for an indefinite amount of time, as long as he is able to, still enjoys it, and it does not interfere with the increased time he is spending on his outside interests.

Ray points out that retirement really isn't what it used to be.

What happened to me turned out to be pretty common, and also very unceremonious. I didn't get a gold watch and a big sendoff lunch. I took a package and exited with thousands of people. It was really the right time for me in my life . . . but it's not like it was for my dad, not a clean break. I'm officially retired from my company, but I'm not done working.

Continuing to work is one of the ways the boomers are redefining retirement. Whether or not they need to for financial reasons, older boomers are finding productive second careers and jobs that complement their changing needs as they age, and their desire to test out different skills or do things they put off in their prime earning years. Ray is not sure if he would have understood all this if it weren't for his computer.

When my company announced it might be offering early retirement—and that "offering" wasn't as optional as it might sound— I really didn't know what to think or what to do. Then my son sent me a bunch of website links, magazine articles about taking early retirement and what it means for companies and employees. I had never really thought about it, but it was clear that this was common and I wasn't alone. I found an employment lawyer over the internet who advised me on my package. And I found the consulting firm I work for now from a chat room of ex-employees of my company! I never even knew this kind of resource existed.

Ray did not feel as strongly as Linda and Jim did that technology was absolutely everywhere. He did feel like technology had made some big changes in the world, and it had brought some discrete changes to his life, but he felt he could get along without it. On the other hand, he could appreciate the extent to which it was influencing the lives of his children, and found himself shopping for tech gadgets for them on gift-giving occasions.

I got my daughter a new portable phone for Christmas last year. She kept complaining hers had a really bad battery, so I got one with the longest battery life I could find. It's really a good idea for her to have it, in case my granddaughter's school needs to call her or something.

But Ray never bought himself a cellular phone. His daughter's old cell phone sits in his car's glove compartment, in case of emergency.

Some interesting lenses for Ray:

• The original is always better.
Ray does not really believe that innovation means improvement. He believes that product quality has decreased a lot since he was a kid.

I have what I consider to be a really nice car. What most people would consider to be a really nice car. It has a lot of technical gadgets in it. It can tell me what temperature it is outside, remember my seat location, cool off my wife and heat me up at the same time! Really amazing. But, I have to admit, I think the cars I had when I was first driving were more solid. They were built better. They lasted longer. They didn't fall apart in small accidents. Though I have become attached to my creature comforts, I also think technology can be used to cover up the fact that the main product just isn't as good.

He also applies this thinking to computers.

When I got my first computer at work, it was oversized compared to what you get today, and it couldn't do half as much as I can do with mine now. But I swear, it never, ever broke, and I never lost any files, and it was just so much easier to deal with.

• Online means e-mail.
When Ray logs onto his ISP, he does so primarily for e-mail. He

spends three times the number of minutes on e-mail versus looking at websites or any other internet activity.

*What I love about the computer is my e-mail. I don't write paper
correspondence anymore. It's so much easier for me to write a business letter to a company than it is to do that same thing on paper
and send it through the mail. And it's instantaneous; I don't
have to wait for days or risk the post office losing something. And,
I would never sit down and write my male friends formal penned
letters . . . but I write them letters on e-mail all the time. I'm not
sure how we got along without e-mail.*

When we asked Ray about potentially buying things online, he
laughed.

*I am not sure that's for me. I mean, how do you make sure your
credit card number isn't floating all around the internet? Plus isn't
it just easier to go to the store and get something? Why pay to ship
things when you can just get in the car?*

• **Definitely believes in Big Brother.**

When we probed a little further, there was a pronounced feeling
that computers and phone lines invite an invasion of privacy.

*I don't get a lot of junk mail in my e-mail box. But my daughter
buys things on the internet all the time, and she actually had to
change her e-mail address because she was getting so much. I don't
think companies have any business with my personal information
. . . but I think computers have made it easier for companies to get
that information, and have lessened the ethics of companies. They
don't really respect privacy anymore.*

• **Prefers embedded technology to pure computing.**

When Ray talked positively and enthusiastically about technology,
it was in the context of making everyday products more interesting. He spent far more time talking about embedded conveniences
than anyone else we followed.

We have an iron that is sensitive to the kind of fabric it's on. And it turns itself off. Of course this means that I can now iron too! But seriously, someone had to think about how we use irons and the real problems people have. And they solved them with technology. I think that's the promise of technology. The computer, on the other hand, while it's a great thing for businesses . . . it has a long way to go before it's really useful for the average person.

• **Computers are very difficult to use.**

Ray continued on to say that for every hour he uses his computer, he feels he spends two hours trying to get one thing or another to work.

There was one weekend when I spent both nights, four hours each night, just trying to hook up my printer. I couldn't understand the instructions. I couldn't get anyone on the phone. When I did get someone on the phone, they were using such technical terms that I didn't understand what they were talking about. Finally, I got my neighbor to come over. He works for a computer company and we still spent an hour till it finally worked! All so I could get a piece of paper with ink on it.

Ray says he is willing to spend extra time learning things about his computer, because he feels he only has to learn them once to have that learning pay off. But he doesn't feel the avenues available to pursue this learning (the instructions, the telephone technical support personnel) are equipped to meet his particular needs.

• **Most computing equipment is very unappealing.**

Because of these experiences, Ray has a very low tolerance for computer shopping.

I know people who go to Best Buy and look at the computers every time. I don't. I go to the music, movie, or camera areas. I really don't like comparison shopping because it's way too complicated. It's even too complicated for the salespeople.

Also, I really don't feel the machines were made with me in mind at all. Everything has to have a different password. All the software doesn't work together. The manuals are really hard to learn from. I feel like all these things are for my kids . . . or people who grew up with computers, who understand them because they are just used to them.

Therefore, Ray "shops" the advertising and purchases simplicity and benefits.

If I need something, I get the Sunday paper and read the store circulars. Who's selling what? Does it look appealing? I can usually understand the two sentences they say about it. Is it going to make my life easy? Can I just plug it in and it works, or do I have to put something together, load something, connect a lot of parts that really aren't going to work without someone giving me a ton of help?

Conclusions about Ray

Ray uses technology if he sees a clear benefit in doing so. He buys into the fact that technology can make ordinary products extraordinary. However, he finds pure computing to be a chore, although he has some online routines he can't live without. He doesn't think the products are designed to suit his needs or learning style.

Avoiding Seven Deadly Traps of Marketing Tech to Boomers

Hopefully this chapter has given you an interesting perspective on the intersection of baby boomers and computing. Some things that became clear to us through this exploration:

Boomers want illustrations of how technology will specifically benefit them.

Younger boomers are more tolerant of "speeds and feeds" driven benefits, but this is not an optimal way to sell technology. If the end benefit of a new computer is better communications capability to improve e-mail communication, or simpler, easy-to-use software, these are the selling features boomers need to hear about, not tech specs.

Not all boomers have the same range of needs.

As one goes through the decades, the needs are more focused, but just as important to the user. Boomers with families at home have an increased need for multiple devices and expanded capability, whereas individuals moving toward retirement begin to focus on themselves and their passions, and their technology purchases reflect these.

Product managers have failed miserably with innovations that do not consider the over-40 user.

Technology products themselves are not addressing the full range of needs of this generation. Simply combining products and services differently and acknowledging changing needs could deliver much stronger brand connection to these consumers.

The internet isn't just for teens.

The online environment is a critical resource for boomers. Providing them with communication and research resources suited to their life stages provides high relevance and value that are worth a premium price.

Boomers are half-awed and half-intimidated by computers.

The same capabilities that make lifesaving equipment so wonderful make home products difficult to use. The majority of boomers perceive computers as taking power away from human beings. They are well aware they did not grow up with such equipment and feel separateness from it in their lives.

Appropriate continuing education is missing.

Part of fixing the technology generation gap is providing educational tools, facilities, and people who understand how to talk with the average person about diagnosing and using their own equipment. The technology industry needs to focus on making boomers more self-reliant, as this has a direct correlation to the individual's brand satisfaction and likelihood to expand purchasing behavior.

Straightforward is better.

Boomers respond to straight talk about their equipment. Clear benefits with attractive packages, a fair price, and brands that emphasize simplicity and trustworthiness are winners with this group. Illustrations of people they know and trust, from the guy next door to a famous business figure, help underscore a brand's paid communications to the boomer target.

8

"You Don't Look Fifty!" What Boomer Women Want in Apparel

Sherri Akers
President, For Women Mostly

S hopping for clothing used to be a miracle cure for baby boomer women. It was the lift that would chase away the blues, an opportunity for socializing. Baby boomer women read about clothing, talked about clothing, and nothing felt as good as wearing a new outfit. They looked forward to each new trend and dressed so their friends would notice.

When baby boomers hit their teens, they created a new market—juniors. Prior generations dressed like children until they transitioned into the same styles that their mothers wore. Suddenly, there was an entirely new way of dressing. Boomers were the beneficiary of an unparalleled marketing focus. There had never before been a demographic that dominated the market in the same way. Department stores dedicated whole floors to juniors. A new category of retailing was born with national specialty store chains such as The Limited, The Gap, Wet Seal, and Contempo. Almost anything that went into the stores in the junior market flew out. The appetite of boomer women was insatiable and their numbers seemed limitless.

The emergence of the junior market can only be compared with the internet boom. Everything seemed to work.

As boomers moved into their twenties, the product direction remained similar as it adapted to improved quality and higher prices. Product categories expanded to career, active, and casual, creating new opportunities.

For Women Mostly, develops a new line of clothing called r.e.d. (relax, enjoy, dream), 310-439-1186; www.relaxenjoydream.com

And Then She Grew Up

As the baby boomer matured, the apparel market struggled to figure her out. It became fragmented. Clothing was updated or traditional. It was trendy or classic. The terminology was purely black and white. A customer was "better" or moderate. She was (the most insulting of terms) "missy," or—heaven forbid—"plus-sized," in which case the stores might not even offer a selection.

Suddenly shopping was not a lot of fun. It was equal parts work and frustration.

By the mid-1990s, the specialty stores that had blossomed as the boomer women's personal playground faced a choice. Should they continue dressing women in their teens and twenties, the age the boomer had left? This would mean shifting to a smaller segment of the market whose numbers did not begin to approach those of the boomer. Or should they adapt their product direction to stay with the customer they had been serving?

Staying with the larger market seemed the most logical solution, but the path was not quite so clear. Our industry was not sure who the boomer customer was anymore. If she was over thirty, wasn't she old? Would sizes 2 through 12 (with an emphasis on 4, 6 and 8) still satisfy her? Was she—horrors—bigger now?

Who Is She?

Manufacturers and retailers can't be blamed for our failure to understand the changes in the bodies of boomer women. The boomer was struggling to understand them herself. She had not necessarily gotten fat. Things had just shifted; a little thickening around the waist; a tummy where she used to be flat. There were now parts of her body that she did not enjoy revealing. Her taste and sense of style had not disappeared. Yet there was a disconnect between what she liked and what she found flattering to wear. She was faced with a struggle to adapt to this new body.

The now older boomer woman seemed to drop through the cracks. Stores made myriad misguided attempts to reach her, most of which only further alienated her. Women who used to haunt their favorite stores now dreaded shopping. When asked where she shopped, she was stumped.

The styles she liked were made to flatter a younger, leaner body. The clothing that was designed to fit her body was—well, frumpy. It had elastic waists and pleated fronts, baggy tops, and tunics that came down past her hips. The industry perception was that if she was no longer a size 6 then she would not be flattered by clothing that was body hugging—in fact, that she should want to hide her body. From the consumer's perspective, the message was clear. If she had lost her twenty-something body then her sense of style was lost as well.

Surveys indicate that boomers perceive themselves on average as 13 years younger than their age. They are fit and active. In many cases, more so now than they were in their youth. Their lifestyle and perception of themselves was completely out of step with the clothing offered.

To add insult to injury, the boomers' wardrobe needs were further complicated by a life filled with multi-tasking. Many postponed having children. Those who did have kids began to find that their kids grew up but didn't leave home. As the kids of boomers began having their own kids, the boomer Mom was often pressed into service with a new version of the blended family. At age 50, the baby boomer may be a new mom, a soccer mom, a young grandmother, a caretaker for an aged parent, or most likely some combination of the four.

Here are some facts:

- 58 percent of women who are boomers are married.[1]

- In 1998, only 35 percent of married couples with children under six had a wife that was not in the labor force.[2]

- As of the year 2000, in 63 percent of married-couple families both parents work.[3]

- In 2002, there were nearly 1.5 million births to women over age 30, a figure that has been rising steadily since 1980.[4] Today, the thirty-something is often the younger mom in "Mommy and me" groups.

- The 2000 U.S. Census shows 18 million Americans aged 18 to 34 live with their parents. A reported 56 percent of the college Class of 2001 planned to live with their parents for awhile after graduating.[5]

- One in four children has a grandparent living in their home—and 75 percent of those grandparents are the head of the household.[6]

Which life is she supposed to dress for? Her own attire may well be the last priority before racing out the door in the morning. You can hotly debate whether it is easier to get a toddler off to daycare or a teen off to school. Technology has allowed work to migrate home with her. Because of this, she feels less guilt about the time taken off to attend a school meeting or run the kids to a doctor's appointment. Chances are she has answered (or at least checked) her e-mail, voice mail, and faxes before she leaves the house in the morning. Her day ends with running errands on the way home and walking in the door to the demands of a household. The best wardrobe is the one that is the most accommodating, in both comfort and ease of maintenance.

Suddenly, the stores that she was used to buying from had nothing to offer her. Moreover, many of us in the industry worried that if we were perceived as addressing the boomer, we would alienate the thirty-something.

The Fix

What we had failed to recognize was that the needs of the boomer were not all that different than those of her younger counterpart. It wasn't just the boomer who was changing—the needs of women in general were changing.

Today's 50-year-old woman has a great deal in common with her 38-year-old counterpart. Either one may be a soccer Mom or have a newborn. The benchmarks in her life relative to children and career play a greater role in her purchases than age. Does she have more time for outdoor activities because she is 34 and still waiting to have kids, or because she is 55 and the kids have moved out of the house?

When I was 30 and my mother was 55 we had very different styles. This year, I will turn 50 and my stepdaughter is 34. We buy many of the same products and have similar styles and needs. We are not the exception!

The clothing industry has to let go of the long-accepted age brackets and instead, think in terms of lifestyle. There are potential customers ranging in age from 35 to 64 who share many of the same needs and wants. That's 53.6 million women—51 percent of women shoppers.[7] They differ based on when they made their choices and what those choices were. Age is not the deciding factor. The boomer is dictating our product direction and success, whether we have recognized it yet or not!

What Doesn't Work

In the last decade, the major marketing thrust in our industry has been price. If we can't succeed in delighting our customer with product, maybe we can lure her in with discounts. This price competition has necessitated a global sourcing approach, resulting in much longer lead times from product concept to finished goods. If there is strong customer demand for a product, it will have an impact on next year's offerings, but rarely next month's. When our product direction is firmly set so far in advance, we make safer choices. Product offering becomes homogenized as a result. Every store looks the same. This further discourages the customer. There is little joy in shopping when it has become largely a matter of comparing prices.

How to Reach Her

The boomer today feels a pride in how she is redefining age 50. When her mother turned 50 she seemed old, but not the baby boomer! boomers don't compare their youthfulness to the size 2 models seen in fashion magazines but to what their parent's generation looked like at age 50. They do not want to radically change their style. They just want to adapt it to provide more comfort and versatility. Talk to her about separate pieces that combine into outfits for work or casual time. Talk to her about clothing that washes easily, dries quickly, and doesn't need ironing. Talk to her about clothing that will allow her to look and feel fresh after a 10-hour plus day of multi-tasking. Don't talk to her about which colors are new and trendy this season!

There is no potential market that begins to approach the buying power of the boomer. We need to address her or get out of her way.

- Almost one-third of women in the U.S. today are aged 50 and older.[8]

- Someone in America turns 50 every 7 seconds—that's 12,000 people a day, 4 million a year.[9]

- In the next 10 years, the 50+ market will increase by more than 25 percent, as the 25-to-49-year-old market shrinks.[10]

- Women 50 and older spend nearly $58 million a day on clothing.[11]

- In 2000, the 45-to-54-year old woman spent an average of $2,371 per year on clothes, 15 percent more than her 25-to-34-year-old counterpart.[12]

As a generation, baby boomers were always the skeptics, challenging authority. They don't follow blindly based on a slick ad. They can appreciate an ad for its style without it influencing their purchase. They want partners. They are far more influenced by a friend's experience with a product than by an ad.

As makers, we need to do our homework; research what has changed in her life and her body, convince her that we know what we are talking about. Every time we sell one boomer, we sell 10 others. She networks. She shares. We each need to find a way to join this community.

The internet is a powerful tool for this purpose, a channel for talking directly to the customer and hearing her answers unfiltered. Who does she trust? Where does she talk to others? We need to find ways to join her in those venues and influence her. We need to hear what she perceives her needs to be and educate her about other opportunities and benefits.

When customers buy a kitchen item, from an appliance to a spice, they often inherit a new sorority. They can go to the product website and get user-friendly tips—help in real time through a chat function; recipes shared with like-minded customers. In the process of providing this community, the maker earns the right to "eavesdrop"—better market research than a focus group or market survey ever provided! Apparel makers need to create this culture, or lose market share to the makers that do.

A great example of this is the site www.jugglezine.com. The site opens to an article that centers on the juggling we all face in tackling the balance of work and life. The articles and illustrations are clever and the information contained is very useful. The site is simple. The user is not bombarded with a lot of places to go. The articles feature links for those interested in delving further into the subject. The few interactive aspects are designed in a humorous manner, pulling her in. It would be easy to miss the diminutive Herman Miller logo  in the upper corner of the site. The site never mentions its products. It never tries to sell them. It provides a service, a refuge from the noise. The company's ability to see where users go on the links, where they spend their time while on the site, what they share with others, and their responses to the one-question surveys allows it to collect an enormous amount of customer information that will help it both develop its office products and market them.

Changing the Design Process

People far removed from the consumer's point of view do the majority of product design in apparel. If the designers are women, they are usually younger, more slender, and more affluent than the boomer women for whom they are designing. Product development and evaluation is rarely done on a real body. The focus prior to the sale of the garment is on style—as viewed on paper and on the hanger. Often it's not seen on a body at all until the product is moving into production. At this point, it can be modified for a best fit but not really redesigned. Even in the production fitting process, it's usually viewed on a well proportioned size 8 or 10—despite the fact that 65 percent of American women are size 12 or over! Pockets that look great on a lean body may produce an unsightly bulge on a more rounded mature figure. Stylish but unforgiving waist treatments are challenging when a woman's weight fluctuates up or down by five pounds or more.

We have rarely had a "user" experience on the product we are producing. As part of the product development and selection, product needs to be "life-tested." If we aren't eager to wear the product, why would our customer be?

It is a huge breakthrough when the market uses a boomer model, but a more important step is when she is shown the overlap that exists between ages. A great example was last year's Talbots campaign: a boomer mother and her adult daughter walking on the beach with a toddler hand-in-hand between them. The outfits worn by the mother and her mother are from the same Talbots collection—showing the ageless qualities of their product.

Where We Go from Here

We need to focus on who boomer women have always been and how that has influenced who they are now. Their clothing is not about trends; it is about lifestyle. We need to recognize what has an impact on their lives and how they needs to dress for their lifestyles. We need to get close to her in order to do our homework. And we need to make sure we let her know that we have figured this out.

This mock ad done by *More* magazine[13] says it all:

"IF YOU WANT MY MONEY, STOP SHOWING ME PICTURES OF MY DAUGHTER IN UNDERWEAR."
And stop pretending you think she's me. That's not "aspirational," that's obnoxious. It's your decision

More Magazine @ 2002 Mary Lou Quinlan. Used by permission.

Adapting to Change

As the boomer adapts to the changes in her body and lifestyle, how do we adapt our product and marketing?

It's all about the clothing

It would surprise most consumers to learn that they are often the first to wear a new fabric, beyond a 10-minute try on in the fit process! The materials used in a garment—fabric, trims, zippers, and so forth—are usually tested in a lab to insure that they will meet standards when the proper care instructions are followed. Among other things, they are tested for color fastness, shrinkage, durability, pilling, and distortion. However, no one has lived with the product. No one has spent a day in it and determined that it doesn't itch, or that the fabric breathes. By the time there is an opportunity to do so, the fabric has been produced in bulk and may well be sold two or three seasons out.

Fabric selection usually is made based on a combination of how it looks, drapes, tailors, feels to the hand, and on price. However, all of these perceptions change when you are wearing it versus handling it. By the time anyone is wearing it, it is a done deal.

A fabric has to be wear-tested; not just tried on, but worn for hours at a time. When we are selecting between qualities, we need to wear-test the same item in each fabric. Technical treatments planned for fabrics may be eliminated because of how they cause the fabric to react on the body. Fiber contents may be changed to provide properties that will make the wearer more comfortable in humid climates. Choices will be made based specifically on what we learn from '"life testing"' the product.

Real bodies

The fit on clothing is generally reviewed and modified on a fit model. These models are a tremendous asset to a maker. They are able to give feedback about how the garment feels and wears. Is the fabric comfortable? Is the model able to move freely in the garment? Does it bind or irritate in any spots? Generally, these models are well proportioned and at the low end of the size scale. Product made in sizes 6 to 16 will be fit on a model that is a size 8 or 10. In other words, she is far from the typical consumer of the product.

As mentioned earlier, more than 65 percent of American women are size 12 or over and most women are not the same size in tops and bottoms. They are rarely well toned and well proportioned.

It is essential that we view our product on a variety of "real bod-ies." When developing a contemporary full-figured clothing line recently, we did pre-production fittings on three separate sizes. Offering sizes 12 to 24, we viewed the product on fit models that were sizes 14, 18, and 22. We also recruited a variety of body shapes from the ranks of the company employees to do try-ons—wider torso, wider hips, hour-glass, round, and column shapes. Yes, this was an added expense. Yes, it increased the time needed for pre-production. However, this focus assured that we were designing for the real end user, not an idealized version of her.

Apparel return rates in catalog, TV, and on-line shopping can run at 30 percent or higher. At least one major retailer acknowledges a 33 percent return rate on full-figured women's apparel bought in its store. More and more often, the only try-on occurs in the customer's home, no matter in which channel the purchase was made. For all the reasons mentioned previously, boomer customers just don't have the time or inclination to spend time in a store dressing room.

By reviewing product on a wider range of sizes, we can skew the size assortment to favor the sizes for which that style is most suited. By observing that a style has limited appeal to most body types, it can be eliminated or reduced in the assortment.

Be generous

Too many choices are made for greater efficiencies, cost savings, or liability protection.

We need to stop specifying hand wash on a garment because we believe our customer will settle for that. We need to challenge ourselves to achieve a care instruction that makes her life easier. Let's not make her live with garments strewn throughout the house to hang dry. Let's work to accomplish tumble dry. Consider the added cost to our materials to be an investment in winning a repeat customer. The first sale is the one that costs us the most. The repeat customer is our real moneymaker. Building in quality is our most effective advertising. The money we spend to pre-shrink our goods will buy us customer loyalty.

Let's not short change our customer by shipping on a size scale that reduces our fabric yield or determine the sweep on a skirt by what will give us the tightest marker. The profits are short lived. If we deliver a size scale that serves the customer who is buying our goods, the increased sell through will generate more business. How often do we see our rate of sale plummet after the most-wanted sizes are gone? Look at the markdown rack. See what sizes are not there. We need to ship more of those sizes.

Let her speak

The customer is dying to be heard.

The internet provides an incredible tool to collect information that could vastly improve product offerings. The first online survey we posted had over 3,000 responses in the first month. Not only did this information drive product decisions, it was a tremendous marketing tool when presented to the retail accounts.

We also conduct consumer "mixers." These are not formal focus groups held at arm's length, but casual get-togethers in groups of 10 to 15 women—today's version of a Tupperware party. Informal modeling (on real bodies!), a luncheon, try-ons, and a gabfest. It is a real eye opener for a design team when they see their product on real people and hear the feedback.

Sell her twice

We have to sell our customer twice. The first time is the impulse purchase, when she orders on line, takes it home from the store, or places the call to order. The second sale, when she decides whether she is going to keep it, is just as important.

TV shopping channels, catalogs, and online retailers have a phenomenal opportunity to "talk" to the consumer about what makes their products unique. This absolutely has an impact on the initial sale of the product, but all of this effort is often undermined when the customer receives the goods. I recently ordered from a line of apothecary products from a TV shopping channel after being very impressed with the ingredients and qualities that were featured. However, when the product arrived 6 days later, all of that was a distant memory. I wondered what I had been so enthused about! None of the wonderful information that I saw on the show was sent along with the product. The print on the packaging was too small to read comfortably, and I am one of the lucky 10 percent who don't need reading glasses yet. I wanted a refresher course to arrive with the product. I needed to be sold again. Yes, it is an added expense, but aren't we better off spending the money to delight a customer and create an ongoing relationship, rather than giving it up in a higher return rate.

Letting Go

Our biggest stumbling block is what used to work. We have to let go of the "tried and true." We need to be willing to view this as an exciting new era.

When the junior explosion occurred, the garment center was populated by a group of crusty old timers, almost all male. They were smart enough to know they '"didn't get it' and they brought in young talent to act as interpreters. We need to have the same amount of vision. We need to find people who understand what our customer is trying to tell us. We need to give them the chance to talk to her. We need to listen to them. Then we need to convince the boomer that we are listening.

The payback will be enormous.

Notes

1. U.S. Bureau of Labor Statistics
2. www.4workathomemothers.com
3. U.S. Census, year 2000
4. U.S. National Center for Health Statistic, Table 68, U.S. Statistical Abstract
5. March 2001 poll by JobTrak.com, reported in the *Boulder Daily Camera*
6. U.S. Census Bureau
7. ibid.
8. ibid.
9. NPD Fashion World Consumer
10. ibid.
11. Bureau of Labor Statistics Data, *Consumer Expenditure Survey 2000*
12. ibid.
13. "The *More* Ad Challenge: How To Sell 40+," *More* magazine, April 2002.

9

Connecting Boomers with Financial Services

Joan Seamster
Principal, Customer Insights

I n August 2001, when Dr. Harris asked me if I would be interested in developing a chapter on boomers and financial services for his book, I was in the middle of exploring the core of financial services for the Dreyfus brand. I had just finished conducting over 75 interviews with investors and investment service providers, exploring what was key to them about money, investing, and the financial services industry.

This chapter incorporates findings and hypotheses from my own primary research as well as findings and reports from other's primary and secondary research. Use this chapter as a springboard for your own hypotheses and for generating your own view of boomers and their needs. Theirs is a market that will not only reward those who are truly in tune with it, but because of its size and significance, understanding and serving it will also serve to change the values and sentiments of our culture.

Boomers are facing the most complex financial services market in the history of investing. Investment instruments have experienced exponential growth. Online technology has facilitated a quantum leap in the available amount of real time investment information as well as analysts' opinions and secondary information. Not that long ago, banks were the focus of people's investments. Consumers relied on their bankers for investment instruments and investment advice. Today, only

Joan Seamster is principal of Customer Insights and an agency principal of Smart, Nice, and Feinwork–Partners That Produce. Contact her at 33 Dover Road, Dover, MA 02030; 508-785-9057; jkseamster@yourinsight.biz or www.yourinsight.biz.

the most conservative investors rely on savings accounts as an investment tool.

Many people become aware of investing through their employers' benefit plans. Forty million Americans today are participating in 401K retirement plans.[1] They are introduced to new investment services when they are presented with a list of options for their 401K plans. At the same time, they are provided with a mound of information to sift through to make their investment choices. For many, this is the initiation into financial investing decision making. Their need to make choices forces them to create some kind of selection criteria for themselves, to develop ways of analyzing financial information. They are challenged to make their own investment decisions. Moreover, the decisions made here are important, since employee 401K plans make up 30 percent of today's retirement income.[2] For many, this is the awakening of their financial muscle.

Higher risk investment instruments are becoming more widespread than in the past. There are both more high-risk products being offered and wider access through the internet to these high-risk products. Over the past ten years, investments in the stock market and mutual funds have nearly doubled in assets.[3]

The younger, Gen X investors see mutual funds as too conservative. They view them as part of their parent's generation. They are attracted by the growth that stocks provide and are willing to take the risk that the stock market represents. The involvement and the experience that the stock market provides also attract them. They want to be "players." In general, Gen X is a generation that is more comfortable with risk.

Boomers Are in the Middle

Between the risk-taking Gen Xers and the more conservative Silent Generation are the boomers. They hold a connection with the previous traditional, conservative investment landscape. Simultaneously, they face the opportunities and challenges that technology and new financial instruments offer them. Some of the more adventurous boomer investors take on the behavior of the Gen X investors. On the other hand, some boomers embrace the investment philosophy of their parents' generation. The rest are left to make sense of the vast array of information in front of them and most are on their own as they work their way through the investment landscape. Whether they are do-it-yourself investors or rely on an investment advisor, most take on an active role in understanding the financial services industry and market place as it applies to them.

At the same time that the financial services offer more choice and complexity, the safety net is being taken away from retirement assets. Boomers face retirement at a time where they hear that they cannot rely on social security the way that their parents have. Eighty percent of boomers do not believe that they will receive a Social Security check.[4] Many boomers are not sure what this will mean in terms of dollars and cents, but they do know that they will have to take on more responsibility for their own retirement assets.

A lack of knowledge

Many workers no longer spend their whole career with one employer. Companies are constantly downsizing and replacing labor with technology, which means that more employees, especially white-collar and service-sector workers, are forced to look for work at multiple companies during their careers. The average tenure on a job today is 4.6 years[5] and the average number of employers for people aged 18 to 35 is 9.[6] This changing employment landscape means that workers have less of a chance of amassing long-term benefits with any one company. What we now think of as traditional retirement with fully vested benefits and a pension will apply to a smaller percentage of upcoming generations. Moreover, as employees leave the companies, many are setting up their own companies and consulting practices, meaning that as their own employers, they are also responsible for their retirement plans.

Today's investor is on his or her own in ways that have never been true before. Yes, there is lots of available information on financial services. However, like learning to become parents, most of today's investors have no formal knowledge base with which they can evaluate the information they obtain. They do not have a holistic view of how investing works. It is a rare investor that has a background in finance or even in accounting. Many take the snapshot of what they understand and act only out of that knowledge, or they try to project that understanding to the whole market. Many see this part of their lives as a train-as-you-go proposition. Some are lucky to come across truly knowledgeable investors who will allow them to ride their coattails or become their teachers. Others rely on the resources available within their network—parents, spouses, friends, life partners, and even financial services phone solicitors—to help them make service decisions.

This evolution in financial services mirrors the transitions in the health-care industry. Cutbacks in health-care coverage and a growing consumer skepticism about the efficacy of the industry have pushed consumers to do their own research, to ask for second opinions, and to be more proactive when it comes to their health care.

We are experiencing a crisis of trust in our culture. We see companies like Enron and WorldCom eroding our trust in corporations. We see celebrities losing credibility and trust through misadventures. Faith Popcorn refers to a trend called "Icon Toppling" where current social order is questioned and rejected. She quotes a Yankelovich survey that reveals that customers will put their trust in friends above experts when it comes to recommendations (65 percent trust friends, 27 percent trust experts, 8 percent trust celebrities).[7]

This is especially true regarding consumers and their investments. Trust is always an issue when it comes to consumers and their money. It has become more of an issue recently. The financial downturn in 2002 made skeptics of many investors. They look to both the investment companies and investment advisors for answers to the current economic state.

The emotional side

Investing is not a purely rational activity. Cultural emotions come into play and contribute to the ups and downs and the timing of the investment market. *The New York Times Magazine* cover on Sunday, September 30, 2001, was titled "The Fear Economy," and contained Paul Krugman's article about how society's emotions can determine the health of our financial markets.[8]

Personal emotions play a role in each individual's approach to investing. The emotional connection between money and wellbeing is especially strong for American women today, in part because it is only in the last century that women have been encouraged to master their own finances.

According to Bob Littell, procrastination is one of the major factors in investing.[9] The cause of that procrastination is in part emotional—fear, denial, and boredom. Financial service people talk about fear and greed as the two major emotions that drive people's behavior. Fear when the market is down and greed when the market is up. As this chapter was written, we were operating in fear. Fear comes primarily from ignorance. Fear can be a healthy reaction to market conditions. It keeps people from taking risks at inopportune times, but it does not allow the market to prosper if it constantly dominates the investment climate. The rational remedy to this fear is gathering information and gaining a perspective. The good news for boomers is that the majority of them are online and have access to a vast array of financial information.

What's Different for Boomers?

Boomers are experiencing these trends and bringing their unique needs and thoughts to this industry in flux. What are some of the ways that they are unique?

As people age, they become more discerning.[10] Boomers are at the age where they begin to experience changes in cognition—in how their minds process information. They retain less information because they are weeding out the non-essential, thus eliminating mental clutter. For them, simplicity begins to edge out complexity.[11]

Many marketers are not eager to communicate to this age group. They feel that this target has already made its product and brand selections and is closed to new information. If you think about their lives and where they have been and what they have learned, it is not that they are reticent about taking in new information. Rather, they are sure of who they are and have the confidence to determine that some information is not what they need.

Part of what allows boomers to take in less information is that they know what they are looking for. They have the basic construct of most of their reality already in place, having developed it over the course of their lives. They are looking to tweak that construct or if the situation requires it, radically change the construct. Nevertheless, in all cases, they rely on information they have already ingested rather than building from scratch. This means that they are more analytical about all information that they encounter. They are also more ruthless in discarding information before it even gets to them.

Think of this age group not as being close-minded, but of being sure-minded. Do not try to overwhelm them with your point of view, because that will push them away. They will listen if you have something that is relevant to them; but you run the risk of being rejected if you don't.

The Boomer Viewpoint

To begin with, boomers don't see themselves as ever getting old, or aging. The current term for this is Down-Aging. Futurist Faith Popcorn initially defined this phenomenon as "baby boomers find(ing) comfort in familiar pursuits and products from their youth."[12] In its current use, it has come to describe a phenomenon where people feel younger than their chronological age.[13] In the case of boomers, it is ten to fifteen years younger. Moreover, they are challenging the formula for the aging process. Since baby boomers crossed the 50-year mark, cosmetic surgery for 51 to 64 year olds has risen 41 percent.[14] This points to a shift in attitude from one of "aging happens" and graceful acceptance, to an attitude of "you don't have to sit by while aging happens" or "aging as we've defined it doesn't have to happen."

In the case of boomers, the sentiment is that they will not react to aging and maturity the way previous generations have. AARP offers a good example of the changing perspective of the 50+ market. AARP recently updated its brand positioning and its on-air advertising. The revamped "Be Yourself." ads now talk about what life means today for those aged 50+. "It highlights products and services that give people choices they want, and the voice they need."[15] To maintain relevance with the boomer market, they are no longer offering some benign view of the graying of America.

Boomer's heritage is one of challenging the status quo. They do not sit by quietly while others provide direction. They like to be in control.

The Boomers Meet Financial Services

What happens when this attitude intersects financial services? We can look to the health-care industry as a model for an industry that is currently being challenged. Boomers have not sat back and quietly watched their benefits and service diminish. How can they? Health is an issue central to their lives. So what have they done? They have taken a more active, personal role in seeking solutions. They are not waiting for outcomes and taking what the medical professionals tell them as the absolute, final word. They are conducting their own background research, especially through the internet. They are evaluating and getting second opinions regarding recommendations they receive from their physicians. They are working the health care system to their advantage. They have adopted a do-it-yourself attitude (DIY) towards health. Theirs is a homegrown strategy of seeking relevant information and coming up with answers culled from the vast array of information provided.

What system or strategy are they adopting for themselves in addressing the financial services market?

Customer service is a central issue for the financial services industry. Boomers' expectations for customer service lie somewhere between Gen Xers and the Silent Generation. They do not have the high expectations of personal service that the previous generation grew up with—expectations based on having long-term personal relationships with their financial advisors. Neither do they have the less personalized expectations of Gen Xers. They realize that the mobile nature of their lives, the turnover in personnel in business, and the shorter-term nature of relationships all point to a changed customer-service experience.

Boomers expect prompt and individualized customer service. The more specific the category is to them the more individualized attention they expect from customer service. This expectation is especially true as it applies to investment services. For boomers, it is not so much about "high touch" as it is about individualization. They want service geared to them. They do not want generalized, mass approaches. Their attitude is one of "Know Me." Their stance is one of "approach me as I see myself, a unique individual who is self-aware." They look for this individualization as proof of the sincerity and integrity of financial-services relationships.

Women Customers

Marketers today are aware of the purchasing power and market influence of women. The importance of women is significant both in the boomer generation and in financial services. Women form a slight majority of boomers. By age 56, the average woman will be single again, having experienced either divorce or widowhood. These singles are facing their later years alone, having earned less than men during their careers, having had fewer years in the work force, and having saved less than men.[16]

It is no wonder that many women feel vulnerable about their financial futures. To minimize their fears and anxieties about finances, they are taking more of an active role in investing. Proof is the growth in popularity of women's investment clubs. Suze Orman, the successful author and speaker on financial investing, embodies what women today are looking for. She has achieved recognition as a spokesperson and teacher for female investors because women respond favorably to her common sense and personable approach to investing.

There is a whole field of study, gerontechnology, dedicated to ergonomics and aging. I mention it here because of the obvious impact that it has on those over age 50 as they encounter, among other things, financial information. Take the issue of type size and the typical financial prospectus. While people over age 50 and in retirement have more time to review financial services information, much of the available information is impossible to read because of the size of the text.

How will boomers affect and be affected by the ergonomics of aging? Clearly more services and products will continue to be developed to enable them to look and act younger. Examples are the newly possible knee surgeries, laser eye surgery, and the plastic surgery mentioned earlier in the chapter. What other products or services are in development that will provide opportunities for the financial services industry?

The situation gets even more interesting when you connect financial services and boomers with retirement. Concerns about retirement kick in when people reach their 50s, if they haven't already. This is the time when people actively begin to look at what they have and what they will need for income in retirement and begin to execute their plan. This is also when people look into the future and ask themselves what they will do in retirement and where they will live. This is a major intersection in people's lives, involving change and adjustments. The underlying financial reality is most people's impetus for action.

Retirement is an individual decision. A person's own *sense* of his or her personal wealth is a key determinant behind the timing of retirement. I use the word "sense" because there is no clear prescription for an individual's financial needs for retirement. Yes, there are formulas. However, one person's "enough" is very different from another's. There are also emotional factors that come into play in helping define each person's "enough."

Although personal, there are some general, universal guidelines for retirement. The earlier generation's guidelines for retirement—stop working around age 65 and change lifestyle to a more leisurely pace, possibly moving to a sunny and warm location—seems to be a fading dream for boomers as they enter this transition phase. (Full retirement age for people born from 1943 to 1954 is now age 66. The peak of the baby boom was 1957. For people born that year, full retirement age is 66 years and 6 months. For boomers born in 1960 and after, full retirement age is 67 years. It may go up even further as more boomers reach their 60s.)

Facing the Unknown

How will boomers face retirement and what are the impacts on their financial-service needs? Facing retirement is an unknown for all generations, but more so for boomers. What is known is that boomers have been less diligent about saving for retirement. About 40 percent have saved less than $50,000 for retirement and only 65 percent currently are saving monthly for retirement.[17] The current analysis is that boomers will create a working retirement, with 80 percent of boomers planning on some kind of work in retirement.[18]

Retirement is not only about the money. It is also about what to do about personal productivity and personal success. I mentioned earlier that boomers are a generation that is about changing the rules. They are too active to just stop contributing. They don't want to be cast aside. They want to continue their exploration and growth, because for boomers learning, work, and religion are measures of a successful life.[19]

Many don't want to make their personal finances their work upon retirement. This is an opportunity for financial services to intermediate or to simplify the process. The TIAA/CREF campaign that features ads with Einstein and Kurt Vonnegut speaks to this attitude. The campaign promise is that TIAA/CREF financial services will take care of your investments while you take care of the things that are really important to you.

What is described is a situation where money is neither the cause nor the driver of people's lives, but rather, money and finances become the *enabler*. People use money to help them explore and define who they are—to afford retreats, spas, adventure, and educational travel. Moreover, boomers will continue to satisfy these needs with the additional income provided by their working retirement.

Grabbing the Boomers' Attention

Rather than consisting of one constant experience, retirement is seen in three contiguous phases.[20] Each of these phases has a different demand and a different impact on the financial resources.

- The first phase is the **Active Phase.** This is early retirement. People are physically active, traveling, visiting friends and relatives, and catching up on activities they may not have had time for during their working life. The focus of expenses in this phase is on experiences. Boomers' focus on Down-Aging means that they will try to extend this phase.

- The second phase is **Semi-Active.** This stage is less active and medical needs are more demanding.

- The final phase is **Sedentary.** Finances and assisted living take priority.

Individuals transition across these phases at their own pace. Physical condition and mental attitude determine that pace.

Making information accessible

What does this all mean to a high-information category like financial services? Recently someone asked me if it would diminish the value of the information if a financial services company simplified the descriptions of its product offerings. Financial services companies often believe that making things complex lends *gravitas* to the category. To be fair, so many legislated disclaimers are mandated that the information often is presented in bulky, non-consumer-friendly communications. In the case of the boomer generation, simplifying the information would be a good first step to take. They will appreciate the direct, clear presentation of information.

A further step would be to become a guide and help them in charting their course and finding their way through the vast array of information. This is advocating a course different from the one that the health-care industry is currently taking. Health-care managers are downplaying the DIY aspect of their industry. They are warning patients about the dangers of misinformation on the internet. Yes, caution is advisable when approaching the internet. At the same time, it is important to acknowledge the drive and purpose behind the use of the internet. Isn't it better to guide your constituents in their search and support their need for information than to ignore reality and downplay the phenomena? Boomers' thirst for information is unlikely to go away.

Courses could be initiated in financial services, in conjunction with other leading organizations, and combined with other boomer activities like travel and fitness. These courses should target not just high-net-worth individuals as do some of the financial seminars on the more upscale cruise lines. There appears to be interest in this area; in March 2002, *The Boston Globe* held its annual Personal Finance Conference and Expo and had its highest attendance ever.

Positioning

The challenge is learning how to communicate to boomers about finances at the different phases of their retirement. For products and services that span all life stages, it is rarely possible to develop a unique positioning aimed at the boomer generation. In these instances, it is particularly important to capture boomers through the tone and manner of the advertising message.

Products targeted at boomers have an advantage because the whole positioning can be aimed towards this group. Qualities of sincerity, authenticity, individualization, core values, and self-fulfillment all are important to consider for tone and manner in boomer communications.

In approaching this cohort, remember to focus on *their* needs rather than acting out of self-serving or irrelevant motives. If you give them what they want and need they will listen. Show them how finances can enable their goals and view of their future and they will be more open to seeking you out for advice.

Do not talk down to them. I recently witnessed a senior exercise class at a local sports club, which was being lead by a young sports instructor. The problem wasn't the difference in age between the instructor and the students. The problem was in the instructor's attitude. He had a fully subscribed class. Yet, he was leading the group while rolling his eyes and letting it be known that he did not want to be conducting the class. Don't give an assignment of communicating to boomers or the over-50 age group to a team that isn't interested in the group, or worse, doesn't respect boomers and their needs.

Branding

Who are boomers likely to listen to in finance? Who is the authority in finance? There are many brand leaders in the industry, but which ones are the icon brands of financial services? (We can define an icon brand in the same sense as Disney is an icon in the family-entertainment category and Coke is in beverages.)

Taking health care as an example again, it is a fragmented industry from a brand perspective. Yet, The Mayo Clinic has evolved into a health-care brand that intersects with all consumers through its publications, at the same time maintaining its best-in-practice status through its clinic operations. Which brands will take on that icon status in financial services?

Who can you partner with as financial services grow their presence with boomers? Picking brands that already have a franchise with boomers allows brands to form relationships far more quickly and, in some cases, more authentically. There are many co-branding opportunities with brands that are part of the boomer's lifestyle.

Disney is a brand that successfully taps into the boomer's sense of adventure and nostalgia. Cadillac is another brand that has invested resources and talent in the exploration of what's meaningful to the boomer generation.

Many other brands have an opportunity to present themselves to boomers in unique ways. This appears to be a time of transition in advertising for the boomer market. References to negatives like "graying" and the problems of aging are reshaping into more upbeat messages about the opportunities of this lifestage. I believe in time that these messages will evolve into more "real," down-to-earth, meaningful statements as advertising connects with the essence of the boomer.

Service

Be believable. Provide services and products that are timely, worthwhile, relevant, and have integrity. In part, this requires developing ongoing relationships with boomers, not just reaching out when the financial industry is in trouble or when a database tells you that it is time for the consumer to renew or upgrade his or her service.

Personalize your service to the smallest group feasible, preferably to the individual. Respect the relationships that boomers have with their money, their resource for the future.

Products

What investment tools do boomers need? What products, or combination of products, can be devised or morphed to support their financial needs? Just because theirs is primarily a DIY environment doesn't mean that there is no room for new financial services and products. It may mean that instead of offering full service, services can be offered á la carte or packages of services can be created to target user groups.

There is opportunity for products that address boomers' longevity and increased financial need that comes with longer life. Products and services are needed that will support boomers' need for increased resources as they enter the Active Phase of retirement. Although not as sexy, there is need for better understanding of the needs and desires during Sedentary retirement, or final phase and for a broader range of products to address this final lifestage.

And, what about financial vehicles to help boomers who are dealing with escalating property taxes, major home improvements, and expensive relocation costs just as they face their more fixed-income years. Just as there are offerings today to help with children's school tuition, so there needs to be legislation and vehicles to help with these other big-ticket items.

So what does this mean? I have sketched some broad implications for the industry. The overriding conclusion is that there *are* opportunities for those who get closer to boomers and uncover some of their needs and connections to the financial services industry. As the boomer market becomes more of a force, more outside resources—research, analysts and consultants—will become available.

There are also steps that organizations can take in-house. Just as they have set up special task forces for marketing to women, diversity marketing, and youth marketing, they can also create a focus for understanding and marketing to boomers.

Understanding human needs is half the job of meeting them.
—ADLAI E. STEVENSON, JR.

Notes

1. Plunkett Research, Ltd., *Financial Services Trends and Market Analysis*, section VII. Consumers, available from www/plunkettresearch.com/finance/financial_overview.htm; accessed July 2, 2002.
2. Presentation given by Scudder Kemper Investments, *1999 Guide to the Generations*, to the Market Research Strategy Group.
3. Plunkett Research, Ltd., *Financial Services Trends and Market Analysis*, section VII. Consumers, available from www.plunkettresearch.com/finance/financial_overview.htm; accessed July 2, 2002.
4. Ken Dychtwald, "The Ten Physical, Social, Spiritual, Economic and Political Crises the Boomers Will Face as They Age in the 21st Century."
5. Dan King, "Reinventing Work (Again)," Career Connection *Feature of the Week*, available from www.jobfind.com/cc_feature_reinventingwork.htm; accessed July 2, 2002.
6. United States Department of Labor, *Bureau of Labor Statistics News*,

"Number of jobs held, labor market activity, and earnings growth over two decades: Results from a longitudinal survey", available from http://stats.bls.gov/newsrels.htm; Internet; accessed June 27, 2002, Bureau of Labor Statistics.

7. Faith Popcorn, "America's Foremost Trend Resource," available from www/faithpopcorn.com/trends/icon_toppling.htm; accessed April 23, 2002.

8. Paul Krugman, "Fear Itself," *The New York Times Magazine*, September 30, 2001, 36.

9. Bob Littell, "Future Trends in the Financial Services Industry and Their Impact on Underwriting," article online, accessed May 13, 2002.

10. Debra Goldman, "Debra Goldman's Consumer Republic: Advice to the spurned baby boomers: Get over it," article on-line, available from *Ad Week*, www.adweek.com/adweek/headlines/advertising_display.jsp? vnu_content_id=1430173; accessed March 19, 2002

11. ibid.

12. Faith Popcorn, "America's Foremost Trend Resource," available from www/faithpopcorn.com/trends/downaging.htm; accessed March 14, 2002.

13. ibid.

14. Plastic Surgery Information Service, http://plasticsurgery.org; accessed Feb. 23, 2003.

15. GMMB, client page online, available from www.gmmb.com/home.html; accessed July 3, 2002.

16. Resource Financial, "Women and Wealth," Library, available from www.resourcefinancialgroup.com; accessed July 3, 2002.

17. Presentation given by Invesco, "You Should Know What Invesco Knows," *The Boston Globe* 2002 Personal Finance Conference and Expo, March 23, 2002.

18. ibid.

19. Presentation by Walter K. Booker, Sr., American Express Financial Advisors, *Marketing to the Pre-Retired & Mature: A Booming Opportunity*, William Paterson University Conference on the Aging of America, November 10, 2000.

20. Presentation given by Invesco, "You Should Know What Invesco Knows," *The Boston Globe* 2002 Personal Finance Conference and Expo, March 23, 2002.

10

The Boomers—
How Do We Sell Them?

Howard Willens
President, Mature Marketing and Research

Our research has shown that boomers are not happy with the way marketers and advertisers treat them. For the most part, they believe marketers and advertisers do not have their interests or needs in mind when developing products, designing packaging, and preparing advertising.

More than one-half of all boomers feel marketers do only a fair to poor job in considering their needs when they develop new products.

Two out of five say marketers do only a fair to poor job in considering their needs when they develop packaging (as opposed to the 4 percent who feel they do an excellent job).

Most damaging to advertisers: almost half of our respondents in the boomer segment feel advertisers and their agencies ignore them in preparing their campaigns (4 percent are satisfied).

This latter finding is consistent with a study conducted by Georgia State University, which showed that the vast majority of "mature consumers" are unhappy with the marketing approaches used on them. Anyone who monitors television advertising and sees gray hair only in commercials for products like Depends, Efferdent, and retirement communities would agree. The conclusion we draw from our findings, as well as from the findings from other research, suggests that the current focus on youth by marketers and advertisers overlooks the size, growth, and affluence of the mature market.

Mature Marketing and Research, 232 Cedarhurst Ave., Suite 27B, Cedarhurst, NY; 516-569-5904; GenerationG@att.net.

In the words of Willie Sutton, it is time that marketers "go where the money is."

Boomer Market Is Diverse

The boomer segment is a diverse market. Its members define themselves not by their age, but by their interests, their causes, and their careers. Boomers are increasingly seeking to make a difference, to ensure they leave a legacy of which to be proud. Further, certain specific, and somewhat selfish, issues are important to boomers, including simplifying their lives, rediscovering their youth, maximizing their wealth, and enhancing their sense of well being. Accordingly, it is important that marketers create an emotional bond (a true connection) between their product or service and the boomer segment, based on boomer attitudes and values. That is, communication needs to build an emotional relationship and speak with boomers in the context of relevant issues.

In short, as marketers, we need to understand who we are targeting, how to best tailor our products and services, and how best to communicate them.

In communicating with boomers, it is important to give them a vision of the future, and not a memory of the past. For the most part, boomers value youthfulness, independence, freedom, and self-expression. However, as with every other segment of society, boomers are not monolithic. Within the boomer age cohort are many lifestyle or psychographic sub-segments, each with its own emotional mindset. Accordingly, it is important that marketers identify the different boomer sub-segments as they relate to their specific products since efforts will be more effective if they target the appropriate segments.

Take one consumer segment as an illustration of the boomer impact. In the beauty industry, an array of cosmetics helps make boomer women look and feel young and vitamins and nutritional supplements promise some of these boomers eternal youth. They don't believe they will ever grow old, and they wholeheartedly believe they will always look as good as they used to look. The communications opportunity here should be obvious.

From another aspect, boomers have set the pace for American society, as they are the first generation to produce financially independent women who earned their own living.

Of all women buying new cars in 2001, 53 percent were over age 40, as were 60 percent of women who used facial moisturizers, and 54 percent of those women who bought computers. Yet, it is a challenge to find boomer women in any advertising messages for these products when you turn on the TV, or page through most magazines. In most print ads and TV commercials, the odds are strong that you will see only young women selling everything from cars to software. The 18-to-34-year-old female demographic is certainly a strong spender, but her buying power is insignificant in comparison with the buying power of women over age 45.

Despite having this information, advertisers and their agencies persist in ignoring consumers over age 40. Moreover, even when they do include a boomer or two in their advertising, our research shows that more than one-half of mature consumers strongly feel that the advertiser did not present them accurately.

Understanding the maturing process is a prerequisite for developing advertising to interest and motivate consumers in the mid-forties and older. If marketers and their agencies pursued their understanding of mature consumers with the same zeal they exhibit when pursuing information about younger markets, their "senior stereotypes" would change rapidly. More ads would address empty nesters, commercials would show older consumers matter-of-factly, and ads presenting "Keeping up with the Smiths," or "Keeping up with John or Mary" as the compelling reason a boomer should buy a product would abate.

Understanding Behavioral Changes

Because the boomer generation is increasingly individualistic, and boomers are heterogeneous even within a specific stage of maturity or a specific age range (i.e., the different mind sets noted earlier), generalizations about boomer behavior are difficult to make.

We need to think more like our target market, more like our gut feeling would have us think. For example, research has indicated that boomers are more likely than younger consumers to respond to emotionally based messages. For that reason, a key to success in marketing to boomers is to place less reliance on rationality and greater reliance on emotional relationships as a lead-in or tone for the product message. That is, first impressions based on emotions are likely to be highly effective with older consumers. However, after an emotionally based advertising message attracts their interest, these same older consumers tend to want more information than do younger consumers.

Additionally, it is important to understand that boomers react to advertising messages differently as they age and mature. Thus, understanding how the older mind processes information differently than the younger will help marketers to achieve greater effectiveness in communication. As an example, boomers are less responsive to information presented in expository style, so communication of technical information targeted to boomers will require a greater use of abbreviated sentences, bullet points, and narrative styles. Some excellent examples of this point have been presented in earlier chapters and additional case studies appear at the end of this chapter.

Boomer Influences

Baby boomers are a breed apart from all other segments of American society.

- With regard to family:
  - Boomers influence and are influenced by children living in the home.
  - Many boomers are still raising and supporting their children now, but will inevitably become empty nesters and with this lifestyle change, their disposable income will increase.
  - Since many boomers had their children later in life, it is common for them to be caring for aging parents and young children at the same time.
- They grew up during the sixties. Many served in Vietnam; others opposed the war vocally.
- Boomers focus on their youth orientation by renaming their middle age "middle youth."
  - Consider the Revlon "Defy It" campaign featuring Melanie Griffith.

- Movies such as *Forrest Gump, When Harry Met Sally*, and *City Slicker* have given us more exposure to boomer trials and tribulations.

Further, boomers differ noticeably from those under age 45 in several basic ways, although they are similar to younger consumers in other ways. For example, a mature consumer is more likely to select a hair salon because the stylist or the ambiance is more important to her than value or price. This reliance on the "relationship" or "ambiance" alone reinforces the proposition that marketers should realize that targeting mature consumers is accomplished best by tailoring creative messages. When it comes to vacations, furnishing their homes, or other categories that give them opportunity for growth or satisfaction, boomer consumers are more likely to spend in greater amounts than do their younger counterparts.

On the other hand, boomer consumers look for value and price when they buy everyday-use products and services, especially in frequent-purchase situations.

Advertising professionals who ignore marketing to older consumers continue to cite two mantras: matures buy price and matures don't switch brands. It is almost gospel among marketing professionals that mature consumers just buy brands they have always bought, right up to the time they become dependent and go to a nursing home. These "experts" do not know, or refuse to accept, the fact that the buying behavior that most distinguishes boomers from those aged 18 to 39, is the satisfaction they gain from their purchases—not price and habit. Accordingly, marketers and their advertising and public relations agencies continually need to be reminded of this and updated about the attitudes and behavior of older consumers.

With regard to the advertising directed at them, the boomer generation has as much receptivity to creativity as younger people do—probably more. Obviously, however, this receptivity comes from a different perspective and culture. Advertising agencies, therefore, must understand that what they may believe to be "great advertising" has little chance of being effective among boomers, when it is produced by a 30-something creative director, using a background of hip-hop music. Pre-testing your advertising is advised!

To compete effectively for the boomer dollar, the onus is on advertisers and their agencies to develop products, advertising, and other forms of communication that are responsive to the lifestyles, needs, and wants of that specific market segment.

For example, the advertising agency for Buick showed little understanding of boomer marketing when it developed a campaign using "Pennies from Heaven" as background music. If Buick really wanted to reach boomers, then music from the 1960s might have been more appropriate and effective. "Pennies," would have been a better selection to attract a market that is older than the boomer—if Buick really wanted to reach that segment.

A further example of the need to develop products that respond to the needs and lifestyles of boomer households is Buick's new minivan-based SUV. The typical customer for its Rendezvous introduced for 2002 has an average age of 53. In accepting the fact that boomers are a separate and distinct market—with distinct needs, wants, and lifestyles—promotion for this newest model will be targeted to buyers between ages 45 and 59. Moreover, if targeted correctly, it would be aimed at that sub-segment of the boomers whose lifestyle, or geodemographic profile, most closely fits the vehicle itself. To us, this sub-segment appears to be, on the one hand, boomer households that have children still living at home or have aging parents, and on the other, the adventurous "empty nesters." However, Buick has not made itself clear, deliberately or unintentionally.

Still, Buick appears to have recognized the need to manufacture cars that offer the ability to transport a large number of people and yet are stylish and flexible enough to suit a variety of family needs.

Marketing and Communication Tips

Marketers should advertise to boomers with sensitivity, using positive images, pictures and testimonials. On an overall basis, celebrities have not been particularly effective as advertising spokespeople. However, the use of older celebrities and models has proven to be an effective way of selling to mature consumers who are more likely to buy a product or service promoted by people their own age. As one maturing consumer commented, "I am offended that someone is trying to sell me a car with a commercial containing models in their 20s racing around, accompanied by a rock and roll sound track."

Some advertisers and their agencies are beginning to recognize that their peers will more likely motivate mature consumers. For example: Gregory Hines, age 53, has been a spokesperson for Total Breakfast Cereal and Discover Cards. Also, Dennis Franz, 54, advertised Cadillac cars; Candice Bergen, 53, was a spokesperson for Sprint Communications; and Tina Turner, 59, represented Hanes Hosiery.

Try to picture boomers as different from earlier generations. They are active, can-do adults with an optimistic outlook—rather than stereotypes of the 1970s and the 1980s.

They see maturity and retirement as a time of fulfillment. Mature consumers prefer to be pictured in an attractive and proactive manner. Your communications should emphasize the positive aspects of mature life. Today's mature shoppers are willing to try new products, and they seek out those products and services that they feel are most beneficial.

Based on the research we have conducted, 70 percent of supermarket shoppers aged 50 and above have tried new products. Successful examples include breakfast cereals that emphasize their nutrition, low-sodium content, lower or no cholesterol, and that are good for the digestion. Also, keep in mind when designing your packaging that men over age 50 are taking on greater shopping responsibility.

Be cognizant of the growing diversity of the mature population. The number of non-Caucasians is increasing at a greater rate than Caucasians. Men are being outnumbered, and financial concerns are more prevalent among women than men. The composition of the workforce is changing. Men are retiring earlier but seeking part-time work. Women are staying in the work force longer. Finally, a longer life expectancy among women than men has resulted in more women living alone.

Other key factors that are often equally decisive in the buying decision of mature consumers include the following:

- Mature consumers' desire for personal growth. This new outlook is described as the re-engineering of the lifecycle. Boomers do not believe that age 50 is the end of their adult life but in a sense, the beginning. Many are even seeking second careers.

- Matures desire to be self-sufficient.

- They seek internal renewal, balanced by social and religious activities.

You May Need a Hook

Youth. Sell them things that make them look and feel young. Boomers think of themselves as 10 years younger than they are, and won't buy it if it makes them look old. Avoid words that focus on age. Words such as "old" and "elderly" are likely to turn off prospective buyers.

Inclusion. Talk to them about the benefits of the product for every generation—for daughters, mothers and grandmothers. Focus product descriptions on the whole family and the variety of benefits the products can provide. Saying that the product is for "adults" keeps it within the range of acceptable descriptions, rather than saying it is for seniors.

Quality and Value. Boomers were raised with a respect for value. They're not penny-pinching like their parents. They just demand value for their money. Educate your target market about your product or service's value, because they want to know. Be clear and straightforward. Matures have been around and have seen a lot, and they don't want to hear another line.

Reassurance. Show your commitment to service. Remove any risk. Just like they don't want to be old, they don't want to be vulnerable. Give them all the information they need to make informed buying decisions. Logically, thoroughly, and emotionally communicate the complete story about your products or services, their features and benefits.

Use Visuals. Keep in mind that boomers are visual. Don't forget that diminished vision is a legitimate problem for this group. Keep lifestyle in mind when choosing graphics and photos. Make it snappy.

Life-changing Events Affect this Market

Life-changing events for this group include: free time after the kids move out; more money now that college and the wedding are paid for; more energy to play with the grandkids; taking care of their parents; returning to education; and second careers.

Heretofore, consumers aged 50 to 64 have largely been ignored by advertisers or else treated as if they were over 75, had no income, or were unwilling to spend what they had. The truth is that, according to the U.S. Census Bureau, those between 50 and 59 have the highest average discretionary income of any age group. Fortunately, old attitudes are finally changing, as companies are made aware of the spending power of consumers over age 50.

Boomers are like an invisible population because they are best reached when they're not overtly identified as the target. Still a certain amount of segmentation is necessary, as suggested below. The best way to address them is not to call them boomers, but to target them obliquely through the interest categories that they have self-selected. Addressing them through their lifestyle interest combined with stage-of-life topics such as estate planning has proved to be the most effective way to reach the boomer population.

Others of the group aged 50 and over are using the internet heavily and in increasing numbers, as pointed out in Chapter 7. They are reported to be going on-line and spending as much as three to four hours a day sending e-mail and researching trips and health information. They are also beginning to use the internet in lieu of their retail shopping.

One example would be a 58-year-old retiree who seeks out websites for new asset allocations. Prior to retiring, he had never gone online. After retiring, he became "addicted" to the web, and now uses it to discover new investment strategies in Money.com and in Kiplinger.com as well as mutual fund tracker Morningstar.net.

A certain amount of segmentation is imperative.

- People in their early 50s may be at the peak of their careers. However, people in their late 50s may be enjoying retirement and therefore have different interests and shopping habits.

- A recent survey identified five important segmentation variables for boomers:

  Activity level

  Discretionary time

  Discretionary income

  Health and lifestyle

  Ethnicity and gender

- Knowing the variables that differentiate your target market and addressing these differences are especially critical to the success of any advertising and marketing campaign directed at the 50-plus market.

Finally, if you really want those age 50 and over to try your product, or consider your service, keep in mind that in addition to identifiable differences, many divergent social and economic conditions characterize that population. Your communications of all types need to reflect these differences.

Case Histories: Communicating with Boomers

Last year, McNeil repositioned its St. Joseph Aspirin to the boomer market. Said Chris Johnson, Associate Marketing Manager, McNeil Consumer and Specialty Pharmaceuticals, "We saw an opportunity to promote St. Joseph as aspirin therapy. St. Joseph, which has always been a low-dose aspirin, was originally marketed to children. Ads today feature active baby boomers. A website is designed to educate consumers on heart-healthy lifestyles."

GlaxoSmithKline Consumer HeathCare is targeting the older part of the boomer segment, distributing Gaviscon antacid samples and coupons to age 50-plus adults. For GlaxoSmithKline, the effort is a "unique targeted promotion vehicle to influence independent living adults purchase decisions," said Traci Plate, Manager of Customer Development. Targeted promotions are important because although boomers do have some characteristics in common, there are many differences. Because of this, marketers can't just consider boomers as one group.

Other marketers are also positioning their products as healthy in an attempt to reach boomers. As reported in *Brand Marketing*, Quaker Oats Company offers the Take Heart line, which includes ready-to-eat cereals, snack bars, and fruit-juice beverages. The H. J. Heinz Company is promoting the lycopene content in its ketchup. General Mills and Dupont created 8th Continent, a stand-alone company that markets soymilk.

"While marketers may genuinely have a boomer-appropriate product," said Courtney Day, Senior Vice President/Marketing, The Senior Network, Stamford, Connecticut, "they have to position it in a way that appeals to boomers." The more creative the marketing effort, the better it will be received. Take the Florida Department of Citrus. It wants to attract boomers' attention by connecting grapefruit with a healthy lifestyle. Working with the Senior Network, it is showcasing Florida grapefruits and grapefruit juice at various lifestyle events.

Aiming at the over-50 traveler, Colle+McVoy, a Minneapolis agency stresses mystery and avoids stereotypes in their advertising. The ads promote exciting nights, exotic locales and romance. As discussed in Chapter 4, the campaign promoting tourism in Turkey is not focused on the young but on their parents. John Nielson, who formerly headed up the agency's division called CODE50, says the campaign is aimed at healthy, active Americans aged 50 or older who have some disposable income and are seasoned travelers. Mr. Nielson said, "Part of what we discovered in focus groups is that it's the whole unknown of going somewhere new and experiencing something different." Another obsolete view about the older-than-50 market that is the focus of the Turkish effort, is that advertisers must cement a relationship with consumers while they are young. Colle+McVoy developed an extensive program intended to educate travel agents on how to develop profitable long-term relationships with Americans older than age 50.

For the *More* challenge, Mary Lou Quinlan, founder and CEO of marketing consultancy Just Ask a Woman, contacted five advertising agencies to create ads to persuade corporate America that targeting women over 40 is a smart marketing strategy. Here are some of their suggestions:

AGENCY NO. 1

The Kaplan Thaler Group Ltd., New York
Title: "THESE BABIES HAVE BOOM"
Concept: "We just think of talking to leaders. They're re-energized, terrific, and self-assured."
Art Director Stuart Pittman added, "I like to think of 40-plus as the cocktail hour of your life."

AGENCY NO. 2

Del Rivero Messianu DDB, Coral Gables, FL
Title: "IN MY HOUSE I ALWAYS HAVE THE LAST WORD ... Yes ... MI VIDA"
Concept: *Luis Miguel Messianu, Creative Director,* sees their ad as capturing the idea that women over 40 are recognized as being confident, in control, and discerning. He believes that there is a need to open the eyes of marketers to Hispanic women. "Hispanic women over 40 can be viewed as the chief operating officers of the household."

AGENCY NO. 3

GSD&M Marketing, Austin, Texas
Title: "SPRING CHICKENS HAVE SMALLER NEST EGGS"
Concept: The way the ad is presented suggests that women have been in charge for quite some time.
Annette Simon of the creative team said, "I make most of the buying decisions, as do my friends. Let's talk to women like they have a brain."

AGENCY NO. 4

"IF YOU WANT MY MONEY, STOP SHOWING ME
PICTURES OF MY DAUGHTER IN UNDERWEAR."

DiMassimo Brand Advertising, New York
Title: "IF YOU WANT MY MONEY, STOP
SHOWING ME PICTURES OF MY DAUGHTER
IN UNDERWEAR."
*Said President and Creative Director, Mark
DiMassimo,* "We asked ourselves what she would
say at her most convincing, authentic moment,
and the ad just lets her say it."

AGENCY NO. 5

D'Arcy, Los Angeles
Title: "AT 42, I STILL KICK BUTT. I JUST DO IT
IN A MORE EXPENSIVE SHOE."
Said Jeff Weakley, Copywriter, "I thought of my
wife's friends. They're vibrant and powerful, yet
sometimes I see the discrimination."

Art from *More* Magazine @ 2002 Mary Lou Quinlan. Used by permission. Mary Lou
Quinlan is the author of *Just Ask a Woman: Cracking the Code of What Women
Want and How They Buy.*

In Summary

Now is the time for advertisers to recognize that although the 50-plus
group represents only 28 percent of our total population, its buying
power is disproportionately greater than any other age group. Therefore it is imperative that:

• Companies develop new market strategies in product development, pricing, and distribution to place special emphasis on boomers.

- Companies make major changes in their advertising and promotion practices to effectively communicate with this group.

- Companies understand what works well with boomer consumers and direct their agencies to produce advertising that will be meaningful to the maturing consumer.

- Agencies give up their youth focus or at least build an internal staff that will be empathetic with the needs and lifestyles of the boomer population.

- On a business level, the failure to address boomers as individuals with wide variations in their interests, values, and concerns will continue to be counter-productive to a company's bottom line. Understanding their individual interests, values, and concerns is a prerequisite for developing meaningful products and effective advertising.

- Baby boomers are a market waiting for companies with the foresight to develop appropriate products and packaging, and for their advertising agencies to develop mature market-specific campaigns. Those companies will benefit from the loyalty of this segment.

- Boomers are in a good financial position now, and they expect to be so later as well. Many are planning early retirement to indulge themselves in the "good life."

- Marketers with an interest in attracting the numbers and economic strength of the mature market to their products and services should concentrate their marketing and advertising efforts on beginning to build loyalty with the boomers for the long haul.

Index

Leslie M. Harris, Ph. D., managing partner of Mature Marketing & Research, is also founder and chairman of Focus on Boston, a focus group and video conferencing company.

Mature Marketing & Research, which was formed in 1996, provides a full range of research services including a quarterly survey of the 50-plus market. Areas of specialization include financial, travel and leisure, pharmaceuticals, personal and health care, computers and the internet, and retirement communities.

Dr. Harris established the statistics curriculum at the graduate school of Adelphi College and has taught graduate school courses in business forecasting at Fairleigh Dickenson University and marketing and marketing research courses at Pace University. In the 1980s, he served as executive vice president at Marketing Research Associates and as ad hoc research director for the Lee Eliott, Bob Launcey and Riedl advertising agencies. His responsibilities included the design and implementation of both qualitative and quantitative projects.

Dr. Harris has served as a research consultant to the American Iron and Steel Institute, the Singer Company, the Junior League of New York, and the Analysis and Programming Corporation of Greenwich, Connecticut.

DAT